Little Known Tales from Oregon History

A Collection of 23 Stories from Cascades East Magazine

VOLUME III

Central Oregon's Quarterly Magazine — Since 1976

Foreword

The collection of Little Known Tales from Oregon History that make up this third volume have been reprinted from the pages of Sun Publishing's *Cascades East* magazine. The stories in this book were originally published from 1989 to 1994.

The idea for a feature on history in each issue of *Cascades East* came from George W. Linn, the first editor to the magazine. He felt Oregon, and Central Oregon in particular, were rich in pioneer history that, for the most part, had never been shared in printed form. He was right.

There are are stories on individuals, families, events, achievements, conflicts, and unsolved mysteries. Illustrated with over 80 pictures and drawings "Little Known Tales from Oregon History, Volume III," like volumes I, II, and IV will keep the memories of the past alive for years to come.

FRONT COVER (Clockwise from the top):

The boat used in the movie "The African Queen" spent a few years as a tourist boat on the Deschutes River in Central Oregon. Sun Publishing file photo (Story on page 65)

In 1934 a raging fire destroyed the original wooden structures at the Hot Lake Sanitarium near LaGrande, Oregon. The hotel and spa was once called the "Mayo Clinic of the West".
Oregon Historical Society photo, #OrHi 39576 (Story on page 70)

The "Beaver Six" car as it appeared in the promotional brochure published by the Beaver State Motor Co. c1914. Photo courtesy of Oregon Historical Society (Story on page 12)

BACK COVER (Clockwise from the top left):

Residents believed a fatal epidemic began in the dining room of Prineville's Hotel Oregon (1901-1917).
Photo courtesy Crook County Historical Society #853 (Story on page 76)

An undated photo of Grace Clark Vandevert whose son William P. started a homestead south of Bend.
Photo from the Clark/Vandevert archives, provided courtesy of Jim and Carol Gardner. Copy of original by Don Burgderfer (Story on page 81)

The Allen School, one of Bend's historical landmarks went up in flames in 1963.
Photo by Don Burgderfer (Story on page 4)

This bronze plaque has graced Pioneer Park in Bend for over 63 years, although some historians now question whether the Clark party ever really came across Oregon to Bend in 1851.
Photo by Don Burgderfer (Story on page 85)

Published by
SUN PUBLISHING
716 N.E. 4th Street • Bend, Oregon 97701

Geoff Hill – Publisher/Editor

Copyright © 2001

Library of Congress Catalog Card Number 88-90788

ISBN 1-882084-05-5

TABLE OF CONTENTS

Volume III

Allen School:
Bend's Own Holocaust

*December 1988 marks the
25th anniversary of the
Allen School fire in which one
of Bend's historical landmarks
turned to ashes.*

Story and photos
by Don Burgderfer

It was probably around 3:30 a.m. on the morning of Tuesday, December 17, 1963, when a loud pounding on our front door woke us from a sound sleep. It was an excited Buck Jenkins who was at our door; and he informed us that the Allen School, all of one hundred yards away from our Greeley Avenue home, was going up in flames. The reddish sky and blowing embers visible behind Buck lent considerable weight to his announcement.

I rapidly threw on some warm clothes, grabbed a camera and joined a throng of 40 or 50 onlookers at the rear of the school. What had been an attractively designed school building—an anchor in this Bend neighborhood for 32 years— disappeared before our very eyes. My oldest daughter, Barbara, had been slated to start school there the next fall, but this was not to be.

There was quite a bit of excitement in the neighborhood. The wind was brisk out of the southwest and was blowing smoke and fiery debris toward homes to the northeast. Many folks were out hosing down their roofs and the Bend Fire Department kept one engine roving the area, watching for spot fires. Ralph Cooper, a head custodian for Bend School District, lived on Lafayette Street about seven or eight blocks away from the inferno at Third and Franklin, but he and his wife remember seeing pages of burned books and papers wafting down out of the sky into their yard.

There was sadness in the schoolyard that night. Ford Hunnell, the school principal arrived, as did the Superintendent of Schools, R.E. Jewell. There was certain pain and some tears, I think, visible in the faces of these men as they watched one of Bend's historical landmarks transformed into ashes. The coming daylight hours would bring much work to these school officials.

This December, 1988, will mark the 25th anniversary of the Allen School fire, and it might therefore be an appropriate time to consider the history of the school and the events of the great fire, a true holocaust for Bend.

Bend in 1931 was not much different from the rest of the country. The Great Depression had a stranglehold on the pine lumber industry of the town and times were hard. But a new school was needed, and the architectural firm of Johnson, Walwork & Johnson (which had designed the Pilot Butte Inn) was called upon to design a new elementary school. The school, to be erected on a site at Third and Franklin Streets, would contain 14 classrooms, a gymnasium, an auditorium and a library. Construction was finished in 1931.

Coincidentally to this, there happened to be living in Bend just prior to this time a gentleman named Herbert E. Allen. He had died October 30, 1929, at the age of 44. Mr. Allen had started out as an accountant, eventually jointed the new Brooks-Scanlon Lumber Company, and rose to the position of Assistant General Manager of the company. In addition to this. he was very civic-minded and had been active in various commun-

Phyllis Graham (l) attended Allen Grade School in the late 1930's. Betty Renk (r) attended the school in the late 1950's. Betty's father, Jim Shiek, was a volunteer fireman for 42 years and helped fight the Allen School fire. Both ladies hold an old photo of the school. It is not known who took the picture (which is now damaged) or who donated it to the Deschutes County Historical Society, where it now hangs. BELOW: A print by Scott Hoyle of the front entryway to Allen School, modeled after this photograph. These prints were distributed by the Bank of the Cascades.

ity affairs, including memebership on the school board. The H.E. Allen School was named in his honor.

We leave it to the reader's imagination as to whether the construction materials to be used in the school were influenced by Mr. Allen's position in the pine lumber industry and his involvement with the school board. Or, perhaps we merely observe a political/economic reality of hard times in a pine sawmill town. In any event, except for some rock facing, almost the entire school, including the key structural members, was built of ponderosa pine.

This choice was to have dire consequences later. But, as one informant told me, "Anybody who, in 1931 in a depressed sawmill town, would have brought fir lumber in from the valley to build that school would have been strung up!"

So, in 1931 the H.E. Allen Grade School was built at a cost of $90,000, using 400,000 board feet of ponderosa in the 330 by 152 foot single story structure which faced Third Street. This Third Street, by the way, was a vastly different, almost quiet residential street then as compared to the frenetic traffic circus we see there now.

Mr. John Jensen was principal of Allen School from 1932 to 1943. He was then succeeded by Ford Hunnell, who was principal at the time of the fire. Ford was born on December 29, 1912, in Laidlaw (now Tumalo). He graduated from Southern Oregon College in 1936 and received an M.A. in education from the University of Oregon in 1956. He began his teaching career in a one room school on the Vandervert Ranch (near present Sunriver). Later he taught in Terrebonne and Tumalo.

A bit after 2:30 a.m. the morning of December 17, 1963, officer Herb Maker of the Bend Police Department was making his rounds and driving north on Third Street. Everything was pretty quiet and nothing unusual going on. He turned around north of town and headed back south. As his patrol car topped the north overpass, he noticed a red glow farther south. At 2:55 a.m. he reported that the Allen School was on fire and the Bend Fire Department sprang into action.

All available engines responded, with one kept in reserve. All 16 regular Fire Department employees were pressed into duty, plus 28 volunteer firemen. Fire Chief Vern Carlon was quoted as saying that the fire had spread so rapidly through the frame structure that there was little they could do to save it, despite heroic efforts by the fireman. Another major concern had been the vast amount of

And why did it burn? What started the awful conflagration? I found out one thing— people didn't seem to agree on the answer to that question.

burning debris being blown into areas northeast of the fire (including the author's home and the future offices of *Cascases East* Magazine). By morning, there was little left to do but hose down the smoldering remains of the building.

Christmas vacation had not yet started, but the 449 students at the school had to start their vacations early. The Superintendent of Schools, R.E. Jewell, announced that the building was fully insured and estimated the loss at a half million dollars. Later, the school district would receive total insurance settlements of $484,578.17, according to the Superintendent's Annual Report to the Board. This report also revealed that during the 1963-64 school year the site on which the school stood was sold to Safeway Stores, Inc., for the sum of $264,000.

The Allen School site had been sold because the loss of the building gave renewed impetus to plans to acquire some state-owned land on the northwest side of Pilot Butte and build a school there. In 1965, the Pilot Butte Elementary School (now called Juniper Elementary) was finished, with the adjacent Pilot Butte Junior High School also being completed two years later.

But, immediately after the fire, there were more pressing problems.

Those 449 students in grades one through six had to have place to go after Christmas vacation, and school officials busily lined up alternative sites. The first graders were accommodated in a separate, smaller buildings untouched by fire at the Allen site—a building called the "Little Allen School." Second graders found space at the Methodist Church, third graders went to the children's section of the Deschutes County Library, fourth grade classes were held in the First Luthern Church, and the fifth and sixth grades were double-shifted into Kenwood School.

Barbara Lutz, a school secretary for many years, remembers the

immense problems connected with reconstructing the student records. Some of the staff initially assembled on the third floor at Reid School to do this, and later an office for Barbara and her principal, Hunnell, was set up at Kenwood, where they stayed for one and a half years. During this interim period, Hunnell was still the principal for his scattered flock, and when the new Pilot Butte Elementary was finished in 1965, Ford Hunnell became the principal there. Barbara Lutz went with him. He retired in 1974 and, being in ill health, passed away the same year at the age of 62. His widow, Maxine, now resides in Ashland, where she enjoys involvement in Shakespearian activities.

Barbara Lutz had spent 19 years with Ford Hunnell. I asked here to tell be a bit about him. She said he was a Rotarian and was very community-minded. Apparently, teachers did not consider him to be an overly strict person, and he was viewed as being quite fair by the kids who came in contact with him. He also was very conscious of how the taxpayers' money was spent by the schools and was said to jokingly refer to himself as "Mr. MacHunnell."

Barbara Lutz said that the insurance company questioned the value the school district had placed upon the Allen School library, feeling the the amount was too much for a "small town elementary school library." But, the librarian, Frances Thompson, had kept accurate shelf lists of all the books, and, because of a freak accident, those shelf lists were not burned. Some of the ceiling tile had collapsed onto the filing cabinet and kept it from burning, as had most other records. Barbara stated that the insurance company took one look at Ms. Thompson's lists and argued no further about the quality of the Allen School library. Frances Thompson subsequently reconstructed her library for the new Pilot Butte School, where she was librarian until she retired.

What was the old Allen School like? Phyllis Graham, who attended there in the late 1930's considered it a lovely school, with large, bright, airy classrooms. It was also located in what was, at that time, a reasonably quiet neighborhood. Betty Renk attended Allen in the late 1950's. She said that Third Street and Franklin Street were really getting to be quite busy, noisy thoroughfares, with lots of load truck traffic going by. She said that teachers could hardly open the windows in warm weather because of the noise. The steadily increasing traffic volume also began posing some safety problems for the children. Was Allen School actually approaching the end of its usefulness as a school when it burned?

And why did it burn? What started the awful conflagration? I found out one thing—people didn't seem to agree on the answer to that question.

People who lived in Bend at the time attributed the ignition to all sorts of things. It was well known that the school used hog fuel (sawdust) as fuel for its furnace. It was also known that the furnace had "blown out" a few times in the past. So, this naturally led many people to speculate that the fire started in the sawdust bins, possibly being ignited somehow by the furnace. One ex-school official told me he first suspected the sawdust bin, but then ascertained that the sprinkler system had done its job well and that the sawdust did not really burn that much. He then told me that the fire probably started because of an electrical short in a motor in the attic.

All the answers I got seemed a little vague and unsubstantiated. Even the Fire Department was unable to help—their records went back only as far as 1970. But, there was one source everyone said would give me the straight dope, a retired Fire Chief whose memory for such things was still sharp: Vern Carlon.

Vern had been out exercising his dogs when I called. His recollections seemed as vivid as if the fire had occured last week. He said that he was aghast at the rapidity with which the building was consumed. At one point, he had just evacuated two engine crews from the gymnasium when the roof caved in. There's no doubt he saved those men's lives.

He said that after the usual inspection he made for causative factors, he had pretty well determined what the real cause of the fire was. But, he also decided to seek independent verification from the State Fire Marshall's Office and called in the Marshall, Walt Stichney, to perform his own evaluation. Walt did so, and his conclusions were the same as Vern Carlon's.

In their separately arrived-at opinions, the Fire Chief and State Fire Marshall determined that a partition had been placed with insufficient clearance near the furnace flue. It was their supposition that a flue fire first occurred, thereby overheating the flue and igniting the too-close partition. Vern said that the tapered burn pattern in the partition clearly indicated the fire origin to anyone trained in the technical aspects of such observations. They also took photographs to prove their point, photos that betrayed the true origin and progression of the fire. And there he rested his case.

One fire expert I talked to said that the use of pine instead of fir in the structural components of the building led, without question, to its rapid combustion and premature collapse. But, he wouldn't let me use his name. Not even 25 years since the school burned down. After all, Bend is still a pine sawmill town, and some of the old boys might get a little testy about that kind of thinking!

BELOW: Firefighters fight the December 17, 1963 blaze at the Allen School. INSERT: A busy shopping mall now occupies the former site of the school at N.E. Third and Franklin Streets.

I Remember The

By Harry Squires

Fifty years ago I was one of thousands of young men who served in the Civilian Conservation Corps (better known as the 3 C's). Although the 3 C's are now long forgotten, my memories of the men with whom I served and of the camp itself as it was in the 1930s are as clear to me as this morning's headlines.

The United States was then in the midst of a great economic depression; millions of family heads were jobless and the country was experiencing a time of tremendous frustration and despair. The Roosevelt administration inaugurated a conservation program to provide jobs for unemployed youths from 17 to 25 years of age. (Curiously, little has been publicly written about the 3 C's and what it accomplished during its brief history.)

Camp Mill Creek

Camp Mill Creek, where I was sent, was located some 20 miles east of Prineville, Oregon, in about as remote a site as anyone in camp had ever visited. The surrounding area was dotted with alfalfa ranches, gigantic Douglas fir, and silent mountains. Most of the men in camp were from the city of New York, with a sprinkling from upstate New York. The hard life of a ranch-hand, a lumberjack, or a construction man was something we had read about, but no one had ever experienced.

We arrived in camp one June evening in 1937 after a bumpy truck ride from Redmond, the nearest railhead. On a number of occasions, the three-quarter-ton trucks were unable to negotiate the hairpin curves up the steep mountains; it was necessary for the truckdrivers to back up and attempt again to get around the sharpest turns.

My first sight of the camp reminded me of a picture postcard. The predominant colors were green and brown. Our barracks, the mess hall, and the other buildings were hewn from logs. A bridge cut from logs crossed Mill Creek, which flowed through the campsite. Over all was a grandeur and silence I had never known.

The first meal we had was just too much. How could they expect a city-bred youth to consume all that delicious beef, gobs of mashed potatoes, pitcher after pitcher of hot coffee, trays full of homebaked bread, and large cuts of apple pie? As I looked around me, I saw men who had been in camp only three months eating as though they were Oregon lumberjacks.

At work formation the next morning, we met the company commander, Capt. James Battle, a tough Army reserve officer; George G. Menkemeyer, the Forest Service representative who was in charge of

CCC

the work details; Dr. Joseph Rekant, the camp doctor, and Oscar G. Hiaason, a former North Dakota school teacher, who was the camp educational advisor. I was assigned to the wood-cutting crew. Our job was to cut all the wood for the camp's needs: wood for cooking, heating the barracks, the recreational hall, offices, and dispensary. We worked in pairs; two men operated the bucksaw, while two others steadied the long log

Camp Mill Creek, Oregon
Photo courtesy of Larry Espey

that was stretched out on two sawhorses.

It was hard work. We had to cut the thick logs into sizes that would fit the potbellied stoves in camp. The first few days I became exhausted after cutting through one complete log; with time and experience I could cut an entire tree before breathing became heavy.

In the mornings when the sun became strong, we took off our blue denim workshirts and worked bare-chested the rest of the day. My partner, Vic Roventini, a big, blond Italian from Brooklyn, and I always welcomed the 15-minute breaks when we sat on the sawhorses while the other crew put on their gloves and manned both ends of the bucksaw. For us, this was a time to catch our breaths and to admire the natural beauty around us.

As the weeks passed and my chest and appetite expanded, I got to know just about everyone in camp—the 200 enrollees, the leaders and assistant leaders, and the camp officials.

Today, after a lapse of 50 years, I can recall the names of many of my fellow enrollees—the camp topkick, Fred Robertson; Mike Mitchell, the supply leader, who was reputed to have been an ex-wrestler; Jack Rosen, who was all of 6 feet, 5 inches tall (in those days a giant); John Kieran, the company clerk; Rudy Bednarz, Bill Illnicki, Bob Snyder and our very capable cooks, Dan "Pete" Peters and "Whitey" Barkoff.

Contests

I can close my eyes today and see the interior of our mess hall as it was way back in 1937 on a typical workday. It is close to 7:30 on a chilly morning. Breakfast is just about finished; men are gulping down their last cup of coffee, carrying their dishes and silverware to the kitchen, and hurrying to their barracks to make final preparations for the 8 a.m. work-call.

The only ones in the mess hall are Sal LaGuardia, the assistant leader in charge of the recreation hall, Vic, and I. We are having our daily contest.

"I give up; ten is my limit," I say as I spoon my tenth softboiled egg.

Meanwhile Sal and Vic are working on number 12. At 15, Sal throws up his hands and concedes the title to Vic, who eats two more eggs to show that he's the undisputed egg-eating champion in camp.

Contests are held in just about every activity. I recall that our cooks,

My first sight of the camp reminded me of a picture postcard. The predominant colors were green and brown.

Pete and Whitey, were invincible in ping-pong. (In those days, the sport had not yet become known as table tennis.) Sam Silverman normally placed third in camp finals, and I would invariably wind up in the fourth spot.

"If I could only solve Pete's bullet serves," Sam would say, "I'd be able to give him a run for the crown."

But other than Whitey, there was no one in camp who could consistently return Pete's supersonic serves.

Another activity in which I participated was checkers. The champion in camp was Dr. Rekant. Every evening I would trudge up the hill to the dispensary to visit my friend, Al Rosenthal, the camp first-aid man, and then to challenge Dr. Rekant for the checkers title. When I left camp in December 1937, Dr. Rekant was still the titleholder.

Saturday Night

Saturday evening was set aside for recreation. We left our pleasant surroundings, climbed aboard the three-quarter-ton trucks, and rode into Prineville. Truth to tell, there wasn't much in town to see. Recreation consisted of going to the one movie in town and then next door to a restaurant for a hamburger and a cup of coffee before boarding the trucks for the ride back to camp.

As summer turned to autumn and the evenings became cold, we would shiver in the back of the trucks as they huffed and puffed their way across the forlorn highway. As soon as the trucks stopped at camp, we would all head for the pot-bellied stove in the latrine to get warm before walking to our barracks in the darkness.

Then the fun would begin. Chances were that we would find our bunks on the rafters or if they were still where we had left them, they would be sprinkled with cornflakes or arranged in such a fashion that it would be difficult in the dark to crawl between the two sheets. This was known as being "short-sheeted." But it was all in the spirit of fun—and what's more, there was no work detail the next morning.

Side Camp

Early in September 1937, the topkick called me into his office and told me that he was sending Bob Snyder and me to a side camp.

"What's a side camp?" I inquired.

"The Forest Service ranger on the Star mail route towards Mitchell," Robertson explained, "has asked for two men to help him during the deer-hunting season. You and Snyder will set up a tent on the grounds behind the ranger station."

"What are we supposed to do?" I asked.

"Your job will be to help the ranger—his name is Harold Freund—weigh the deer brought in by the hunters and to issue and check the necessary papers."

A truck deposited Bob and me, tent equipment, and enough food to last one week behind the ranger station. We managed to get the tent up before darkness set in. That night we had a paper-sack supper brought with us from camp.

The following morning, a clear beautiful Sunday, we awoke with appetites made keener by the crisp autumn air. As I started to make the morning pot of coffee, I became aware of a pleasant aroma from the ranger station. In a few moments the ranger came into our tent and gave us the best news we could have hoped for.

"Boys, Mrs. Freund and I would like you to join us for breakfast," he said.

"What is that aroma that smells so good, Mr. Freund?" Bob asked.

"That is Mrs. Freund's own special brand of home-made biscuits," he replied.

"We accept," I quickly said.

To this day I can smell the aroma and enjoy in my mind that Oregon breakfast of scrambled eggs, hash-browned potatoes, home-made biscuits, jam, and many pots of hot, delicious coffee.

When we returned to the main camp at the end of the deer-hunting season, the old-timers had completed their six-months' hitch and had left for the East. Another group soon arrived; now we were the veterans in camp.

Civilian Conservation Corps Company 6417 at Camp Mill Creek. Photo courtesy of Larry Espey

"The Mill Creek Chronicle"

Mr. Hiaason, the camp educational advisor, called me into his office one day late in September. He was looking at my personnel folder.

"Harry, how would you like to edit our newspaper?" he asked. "I see you've taken courses in journalism and have expressed an interest in newspaper work. The job carries a rating of assistant leader."

"I'd be happy to accept the job, Mr. Hiaason," I immediately replied.

Assistant leaders were paid $36 a month, $6 more than an enrollee. Of this amount $22 was sent home and the CCC member kept the remainder for his personal needs.

Our paper was called "The Mill Creek Chronicle." It was a four page, mimeographed weekly. My job was to gather all the news, write the stories, cut the stencils, operate the mimeograph machine, and distribute the papers. In addition, the position required that I keep the recreation hall clean and organize evening classes in English and arithmatic. (A printed newspaper, published weekly in Washington, D.C., covered national CCC news. This paper was called "Happy Days.")

The weeks continued to pass. The paper kept me busy from morning until after supper. One Sunday after lunch, someone suggested that we go for a long hike.

We followed the highway east towards Mitchell. After a few miles, we left the highway and set out into the forest to the north. About two hours later, we beheld a sight that I shall never forget. There before us was a real, honest-to-goodness ghost town, complete with dance hall, hotel, and blacksmith shop. It was readily apparent that no one had set foot in this town for decades. We walked up and down the one street. Suddenly I heard a shout. I recognized the voice. It was my buddy, Al Rosenthal, the camp first-aid man.

"Harry, come here!" he shouted. "Look what I've found!"

I found Al in a dilapidated shack staring at the ceiling.

"What is it, Al?" I inquired.

"Look at the headline in this newspaper," he said, pointing to a yellowed sheet.

I twisted my head and read aloud the headline: "DEWEY CAPTURES MANILA BAY."

It was a San Francisco newspaper.

I could not make out the month or the day, but the year was 1898. Al, a photographic bug, cursed mildly.

"Why didn't I bring my camera? What a picture this would be!"

Of course, the next edition of "The Mill Creek Chronicle" carried a long article on the ghost town and on our interesting findings.

Shortly after Christmas 1937, our group left camp and rolled down the mountain in trucks. We headed for Redmond, Oregon, boarded a train, and arrived at Camp (now Fort) Dix, New Jersey, where we received our discharges four days later.

From March 1933, when the CCC program was started, until 1940, more than 2.25 million young men were enrolled in 1500 camps in every state of the nation. These men built bridges, fire towers, fire trails, emergency roads, and recreation facilities. In addition, they checked erosion and played a vital role in the conservation of wildlife.

The 3 C's is an almost forgotten episode in recent American history. It was a comparatively brief—but productive—era in the development of our nation's youth—and I am happy that I was a small part of it.

The Fate of the Beaver Automobile

A story of how a small group of local entrepreneurs turned high hopes of financial gain into utter disaster for many of Portland's most respectable citizens.

By Louis S. Schafer

For many people the circumstances surrounding the design and construction of the Beaver automobile, produced in Gresham, Oregon, is a story of corporate incompetence and disorganization; a story of how a small group of local entrepreneurs turned high hopes of financial gain into utter disaster for many of Portland's most respectable citizens. Few understand, however, that the history of the Beaver automobile also involves the story of a courageous attack on the competitive world of the horseless carriage, which would inevitably be dominated by the Big Three auto makers: Ford, General Motors, and Chrysler.

The primary moral to be learned from this story of economic poor planning is that outside forces often influence the success or failure of small businesses. Indeed the formulation of the Beaver automobile concern, along with its subsequent demise, could not have been predicted.

The decision to enter the automobile

ORIGINAL BEAVER SIX·CAR

THIS CAR HAS BEEN ON THE STREETS OF PORTLAND SINCE OCTOBER, 1912

The "Beaver Six" car as it appeared in the promotional brochure published by the Beaver State Motor Co. c1914.   Courtesy of Oregon Historical Society.

manufacturing industry during the second decade of the 1900s came only after a lengthy study concerning the condition of Northwest Oregon's potential growth, business atmosphere, and transportation needs. Population statistics proved that the number of people living within the city limits of nearby Portland had been growing steadily since its incorporation in 1851, and that it was expected to increase even further.

Perhaps, the need for an improved mode of travel in and around the Portland/Gresham area was the most obvious reason to enter the automobile manufacturing field. Local journeys required the use of a horse-drawn buggy, wagon, or sleigh in the wintertime. Today, few of us can truly appreciate the typical rural family of yesteryear, which existed in virtual isolation. Their movements were severely restricted by the distance they were able to traverse in a single day. Usually, this amounted to no more than 10 to 12 miles per outing.

Whenever an urbanite wished to travel any distance outside of the Portland area, he or she was faced with a limited number of options. One choice was daily stagecoach transportation, which had been established between Portland and Sacramento, California, in 1860. Furthermore, since the mid-1860s, railroad companies had begun laying down north/south track routes running west of the Cascades until, eventually, a huge network of lines was completed. And, as a third option, steam ship lines ran regularly from Portland to San Francisco and other points all up and down the coast.

However, there remained one major problem for would-be travelers: they were forced to plan their journeys around specific destinations. Hence, there was little freedom when it came to traveling to other, less populated regions of the west. For that reason, locals began to investigate the advantages of personalized transportation.

After months of discussion and debate, during which a handful of investors studied the vast potential of the horseless carriage, it was decided that an automobile production plant was not only a possibility, but a necessity. The resulting corporation, which would become known as the Beaver State Motor Company, grew out of a partnership established in the late fall of 1915.

The actual organizer of the Gresham-based firm was P.A. Combs, who resided in nearby Portland. Combs was no stranger to the business world, for he had formerly been the vice-president of an auto-supply company in that city. During that time, he had tinkered with the idea of designing and constructing his own version of the horseless-carriage.

First on Combs' agenda was to decide which mode of power to incorporate: steam, electricity, or petrol. In recent times, steam and electricity each had had their advocates; yet, each had also showed their unique shortcomings. Steam, which was actually "external" combustion, required a rather large boiler and water tank, and was somewhat complex to operate and maintain. Futhermore, its cumbersome machinery would subtract from the vehicle's desired spaciousness.

An electric vehicle, on the other hand, demanded the installation of heavy accumulators in order to provide even the most modest of ranges. Its reputation as a "town car" would defeat the primary purpose of the inventor: to build a vehicle which would accommodate lengthy journeys to and from

outlying regions of the city. Thus, Combs came to realize that an internal combustion gasoline engine would best suit his purposes.

The original Beaver prototype automobile was completed during the winter portion of 1914. It possessed a six-cylinder engine, designed and built by Combs himself, which boasted a maximum rating of 45-horsepower. This high-powered motor, which was nestled comfortably on a reinforced steel frame beneath the vehicle's front bonnet, would enable the car to climb steep grades and traverse deep ravines with ease.

Combs unveiled his creation at a business meeting the following year, promoting the car's vast potential to a select group of financial friends. He urged them to take stock in the fact that the horseless carriage was here to stay, and that the Portland area should "join the bandwagon" of entrepreneurs already in the automobile manufacturing business. Those in attendance must have taken Combs' scheme seriously, for, early in 1916, the Beaver State Motor Corporation was incorporated at $500,000 worth of capital.

Not wanting to construct a wide array of diverse motor-cars, which might spread their assets too thin, the investors of the firm decided to stick to Combs' original design, agreeing to fund the research and development of a rather conventional, yet dependable, vehicle: an assembled six-cylinder, five-passenger touring car.

Thus, the Beaver State Motor Company approached their first year of business as one of northwest Oregon's largest corporations. Backed by large sums of local money and organized on a smaller scale along the same lines as the Big Three auto makers, the officers and directors looked toward a promising future.

A plan for gradual future expansion into other states, such as California, Washington, and Utah, was soon formulated. The idea was based on two premises: Not only were Americans throughout the Northwest becoming totally enthralled with the concept of personalized transportation, but the officers at the Beaver State Motor Company believed that the entire Willamette Valley would long remain predominantly agricultural. Therefore, the wants of the leisurely travelers, along with the business needs of farmers and postmen, would be satisfied by the Beaver automobile.

The earliest models of the Beaver automobile, which went into full-scale production during the latter portions of 1916, was certainly a beauty to behold. Weighing in at just over 2,000 pounds, the coachwork stretched itself snugly over a lengthy wheelbase. It possessed

BUILDING No. 1—BEAVER STATE MOTOR COMPANY'S PLANT, GRESHAM, OREGON.
(From Photograph Taken March 7, 1914)

The first unit of the Beaver Plant as it appeared in the promotional brochure. Courtesy of Oregon Historical Society.

quarter-circle wheel protectors in the front, with wide running boards leading back to half-moon fenders in the rear. In order to accommodate the rugged, pitted roadways of the region, the car sat high off the ground in a "buggy" fashion and featured reinforced double-drop steel framework. To further add to passenger comfort, four heavy-duty full-eliptic springs were installed at the corners.

Nonconformity did not end there, however, for there was no typical drive-shaft beneath the car's top shell. Instead, a "worm drive" had been installed between the reinforced framework, which was a form of final drive incorporating helical worm screw gears in place of the more conventional bevel gears. Interestingly enough, the unique apparatus made the Beaver automobile one of the first pleasure cars in the United States to be constructed with standard equipment imported from Europe. The distinct worm drive gear, which had proven its dependability in a number of foreign-made cars, was supplied by the Daimler-Lanchester Motor Car Company of Coventry, England.

In the greater Portland/Gresham area, where the cost of living was much higher than eastern and midwestern states, unassembled parts from all over the United States and overseas were shipped in with an often astounding pricetag. This, coupled with the fact that World War I quickly created a shortage of valuable items, cut heavily into the profits of the Beaver State Motor Company. Hence, the officers were faced with a crucial, yet necessary, adjustment: they raised the price of their automobile.

As the cost of Beaver State's product

The primary moral to be learned from this story of economic poor planning is that outside forces often influence the success or failure of small businesses.

was forced upward toward the $3,000 range by uncontrollable economics, public interest quickly became virtually nonexistent. The seemingly bright future for the locally-produced car was literally being strangled by lower-priced automobiles and predicted expansion came to an agonizing standstill. To put it bluntly, by the beginning of the 1920s, investment capital was lost to the tune of thousands of dollars because there simply was no demand for the higher-priced Beaver automobile.

The Beaver State Motor Company would eventually branch out to design other innovative road machines, including a two-seat roadster and a typically-styled sedan. Combs, in fact, had earlier constructed a small 2.84-meter wheelbase, four-cylinder gasoline-powered utility truck, which would remain in production for less than a year. There was even talk of building a similar electrically-propelled unit, though the innovative vehicle never even reached its prototype stage.

As a result of inadequate promotions, less than a dozen complete Beaver automobiles were sold during the 7-year lifespan of the firm. Furthermore, it soon became apparent that the com-

pany's directors had overestimated the potential for such a vehicle.

Though they were forced to cease automobile production at the beginning of the 1923 season, the Beaver State Motor Company remained solvent. For the next several years the firm manufactured an assortment of products, including sewer pipe, metal castings, rail car wheels, cement mixers, and six-cylinder automobile engines. In the meantime, Combs and the other company officials hoped that one day they would be able to re-enter the automobile manufacturing arena.

Between 1923 and 1929, a number of automobile and truck dealerships opened their doors for business in nearby Portland, selling electric-, steam-, and gasoline-powered vehicles. Since they had been assembled elsewhere, and had been shipped in by rail, cost was held to a minimum: they ranged in price from $700 to $2,600. Thus, the last ray of hope went dim for the founders of Gresham's only automobile manufacturing concern, which could not compete with the importation of models pouring out of Detroit, St. Louis, and Chicago.

The inevitable fate of the Beaver State Motor Company would remain a gloomy memory in the minds of local investors for many years to come. Still, we should not forget the courage and fortitude of those involved in the design and construction of one of the only horseless-carriages in northwest Oregon's lengthy history. If not for the immense economic competition within the auto industry, which remained intense and fatal to the vast majority of concerns for the next several years, their dream might have been transformed into reality.

Miss Johnston

*Teaching school in a
one-room schoolhouse
near Prairie City in the 1930s
was no easy job . . .*

By Dorsey Griffin

In 1936 the local school board for District No. 51 on Jeff Davis Creek hired a non-local school teacher. Patricia Johnston was 21, just graduated from Mount Angel Normal School, and was a serious, well-educated and cultured young woman. My father, then chairman of the school board, arranged for her employment.

According to the custom in rural America, the teacher of a small country school roomed and boarded with one of the local farm families. In this case, Miss Johnston lived with us, the Griffins, in our small but comfortable house.

Patricia was a bit nervous by nature, shy and a little piqueunish ... not that I blame her. She was not accustomed to living with strangers, especially in such remote and close domestic circumstances. She was a long way from her home and her family. And whether or not she ever knew it I do not

Patricia Johnston and her grade school pupils, Grant County School District No. 51, 1938. Teacher in back, Glen and Betty Pierce, the Harrell boys, and my sister Carol Griffin. That's Blackie in the foreground. Photo courtesy of Dorsey Griffin.

know, but wild uproar broke loose in the neighborhood when some of the neighbors learned that she was Catholic. This was on Jeff Davis Creek, remember. During the Civil War southern sympathizers worked the creek banks for gold and some of them stayed to homestead in these hills and their descendents were still in them. One neighbor tried to get the school district consolidated with Prairie City's in order to break her contract.

Once in a while Patricia and I would have a little spat. One morning we woke up to a new snowfall - two full feet of soft, wet whiteness that blanketed the earth. After I had gotten up and started the fires and broken the ice off the top of the water pail, I was to go out and shovel the path to the outhouse. In the early morning traffic in the kitchen, after the water had gotten warm, I had started to wash before I got going. Patricia had

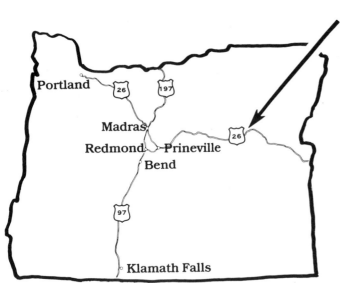

**Prairie City
Jeff Davis Creek**

According to custom in rural America, the teacher of a small country school roomed and boarded with one of the local farm families. In this case, Miss Johnston lived with us

wished to wash first and we had words. My father, as he should have, took her side and "shagged me out" to shovel the walk. And he told me hurry, because "Patricia has to go."

I shoveled a neat, wide path from the back porch of the house halfway to the outhouse. Then I made a flying leap as far as I could jump and continued shoveling from there to the door of the toilet. I jumped back over the unshoveled section, grabbed my lunch pail and hurried to the gate to await the school bus.

Well, of course, Pat got a lot of snow in her slippers and on her stockinged legs. She came back to the house relieved but crying and showed my father what a rotten trick I had played on her ... to dig a neat, wide trench with sides straight up and down but with an unexcavated stretch just long enough to require her to put each foot down once into the deep wet snow that *"cam' aboon her bonnie knee."*. With me out of sight and gone to school, all my father could do was humor her and help her laugh it off, because he was laughing too.

Pat was a responsible and beautiful young woman far from all that was dear and familiar to her. She and her husband in Alaska were to visit my parents and write to them for all these years since. In a letter from Pat, January 1986, she recalled her experiences as a young school teacher in her first job teaching in a one-room, all-grades country school along old U.S. Highway 26, living with a farm family in the 1930s. Pat wrote:

"Living with your folks was delightful. Your mother and dad were so good to me, and so were you and the girls.

The little school was really lovely, with maple floors and curtains on the windows, and a big wood stove to warm us and heat our water, soup and chocolate. I remember the entrance room had a bucket of water to drink and water to wash in. The spring was on the school grounds. So was the shed for the horses. Betty and Glen Pierce came in a sleigh.

Sometimes I would watch the kids in class and they would scratch and find a tick. It made me uneasy, because I did not have the shot to prevent tick fever.

I'll never forget the Christmas program we gave. The school was filled to the brim. I didn't know there were that many people around. That Christmas your mother gave me two lovely linen handcrocheted handkerchiefs. I have them still and treasure them.

Nor will I forget the night the cougar jumped on the roof of the house. The next morning we saw his tracks in the snow. I didn't venture out at night for a long time after that.

Your dad was so good to us. He'd take us to the skating rink on Friday nights in zero weather and wait for us. I remember we rode in the open-air 'Stanley Steamer,' as we called your little Overland touring car.

It was a very happy year with your folks. It was the first and only time I lived on a farm."

Pat (Johnston) Rhodes
Wrangle, Alaska.

Patricia did not know, perhaps, the reason for the large turnout to her Christmas play and program. The neighbors for miles around were curious to see for themselves what this real, live, *Catholic* schoolma'rm was all about.

They were very pleased.

Suffer The Little Children

*An account of one of the most
terrible experiences ever
encountered by an Oregon
wagon train.*

By Eugene E. Luckey

The way west by wagon train was not only difficult, it was extremely dangerous. Danger came in many forms: gunshot wounds, unruly horses and cattle, disease, drowning, and starvation to name a few. It has been estimated that between 35,000 and 45,000 people died on the covered wagon trail west — a grave for every 80 yards of trail from the Missouri River to the Willamette. The flood of westward emigrants started in 1842 when 112 people left Independence, Missouri for Oregon. It continued until the early 1900's with most of the early pioneers making the trip between 1842 and 1870.

Indians along the Oregon trail seldom killed until the 1860's, when the Indian finally realized that the white man was coming into his country in never-ending numbers and his way of life and livelihood was threatened. The following is an account of one of the most terrible experiences ever encountered by an Oregon wagon train.

On September 7, 1860, a wagon train consisting of eight wagons and 54 people left Ft. Hall, Idaho, escorted by Colonel Howe and 21 cavalrymen. The train had with it the customary cattle and spare oxen which the older children drove along behind the company. Colonel Howe had deployed his cavalrymen approximately 100 yards out from either side of the train with four soldiers riding ahead as scouts. The women drove the wagons and the men walked alongside the oxen encouraging them onward with whip and rocks thrown at their flanks. The terrain was mostly gentle rolling hills, there were little or no trees or brush. Mostly it was just stunted sagebrush growing in rocky volcanic soil.

The train traveled slowly—about two miles an hour—the average for a typical train with wagons and cattle. They were following the worn trail of the many trains that had preceded them down along the south side of the Snake River. The morning air was still cool as it was approaching fall, but as the sun rose in the sky, it began to warm rapidly. Dust rose from the animals' hooves and the wagon wheels. It was swirled around by gentle gusty winds to settle on everything outside and inside the wagons.

At night the settlers would circle their wagons so the soldiers could come inside and spend the night within the confines of the wagon enclosure. Cooking fires were small and quickly allowed to go out, as there was little fuel to keep them burning. After the fires had gone out and the sun set, everyone started putting on more clothing, as it cooled down quickly after nightfall.

After the train and soldiers had traveled six days west of Ft. Hall, Colonel Howe called a conference for the men on the train and said, "Men–the army has been patrolling the area around Raft river and the California trail south. There doesn't seem to be any hostile Indian activity. Soldiers from Oregon have been patrolling their part of the trail this summer. I believe that you will be all right from here on westward. We are going to leave you now. Good luck and God speed."

The Colonel knew that the Oregon Department had troops patrolling in the vicinity of Boise during the summer and he believed the trail southward to California was the most dangerous. This was indeed the case. Colonel Wright of

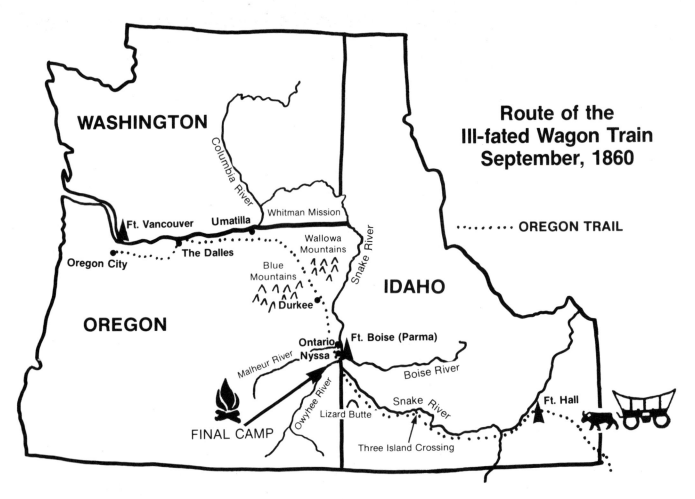

Route of the Ill-fated Wagon Train September, 1860

WASHINGTON

OREGON

IDAHO

Columbia River

Ft. Vancouver　Umatilla　Whitman Mission

The Dalles

Oregon City

Wallowa Mountains

Snake River

Blue Mountains

Durkee

Ontario

Nyssa

Ft. Boise (Parma)

Malheur River

Boise River

FINAL CAMP

Owyhee River

Lizard Butte

Snake River

Three Island Crossing

Ft. Hall

·········· OREGON TRAIL

the Oregon Department had reported to his headquarters on September 20th that the "routes of immigration were rendered perfectly safe" by the operation of troops during the summer. Major Grier's command, which had been patrolling on the road to Boise to look after the immigration during the summer, had just returned to Walla Walla in September.

The people of the train thanked the Colonel and his soldiers for riding with them and offering them protection. After good-byes had been expressed, the soldiers headed back to Ft. Hall.

The wagon train continued on its westward journey. People and animals were tired from the continual traveling, as they had been on the trail since June. Every man, woman and child looked forward to reaching the Oregon destination where they could finally get a long rest.

The train had been on the trail for two weeks since Colonel Howe and his troops had left them to return to Ft. Hall. They were traveling between Salmon Falls and Ft. Boise when, on the morning of September 13, 1860, between 9 and 10 o'clock, 100 Indians attacked. They surrounded the train yelling like demons as they attempted to stampede the cattle herd. The people of the train were faced with two tasks: to corral their animals and prepare to defend themselves against the Indian attack.

The men and older children got the cattle under control quickly and the company was making preparations to fight. When the Indians saw this, they made signs of friendship and of being hungry. The pioneers believed that further trouble might be averted if they gave them food. They allowed the Indians to come in closer and gave them presents of food. After eating, the Indians allowed the train to continue on its way.

As soon as the train was out in the open the Indians attacked them once again, this time firing rifles and sending many arrows towards the wagons. The train again halted and secured their cattle, but before this was accomplished, three men were shot down by the attackers.

The battle continued for the remainder of the day and several Indians were killed by the defenders. The savages' rifle fire was mostly inaccurate; it did little harm except to agitate the horses and cattle, who were already nearly uncontrollable for lack of food and water.

All night long the Indians fired random shots. On the morning of the second day of the attack, they began the battle again, continuing into the second night. During this second day another white man was killed.

Towards sunset the members of the train gathered for a conference and agreed they should leave four wagons to the Indians, hoping they were more interested in their property than their lives. If the Indians paused long enough to pillage the wagons that were to be left behind, the company might be able to escape with the other four wagons.

The next day they started on westward with four wagons and the cattle, leaving the other four wagons to be plundered by the savages. But the Indians paid no heed to the abandoned property and continued their pursuit.

Once more they attacked the wagons while the drovers in the company tried to keep the livestock moving ahead; but, in spite of their best efforts, the hungry creatures would stop and snatch a mouthful of food. This made forward travel agonizingly slow.

With the train were four young men who were discharged soldiers from Ft. Hall. They were well armed with rifles and revolvers belonging to the train, and were mounted on good horses. They were instructed to ride ahead and keep the trail open. Instead of doing their duty and assisting in protecting the company, they fled with the horses and the arms.

The emigrants crept along at a slow pace with the remaining four heavily-loaded wagons. They were still under sporadic attack by the Indians who continued to trail them. The Indians knew they could stay out of range of the settlers' rifles and kill them one by one as killing opportunities were presented. The children huddled down in the wagon beds and cried in fear as they jolted and bounced along the rough trail. Fear for the children's safety froze in each mother's breast as they tried to comfort the children during each attack. Fear, anger, and hope were with each man as he tried to hurry his wagon forward in the ruts of the trail. Each man hoped that the Indians would eventually tire of their pursuit of the train and ride off leaving them alone.

The traveling attack continued until the train stopped again and a conference held. It was decided that because of their slow pace they should abandon the remainder of the wagons and the cattle to save their lives. The settlers salvaged a few things from the wagons and proceeded on foot. As soon as they were away from the protection of

Fear, anger, and hope were with each man as he tried to hurry his wagon forward in the ruts of the trail. Each man hoped that the Indians would eventually tire of their pursuit of the train and ride off leaving them alone.

the wagons, two people, John Myers and Susan Utter, were shot dead. Mr. Utter, father of Susan, made signs of peace, but was shot while proposing a treaty. Mrs. Utter refused to leave her dead husband and she along with her boy and two of her girls were killed. Eleven people had now been killed, six others had left the train, and there remained 37 men, women, and children.

By walking all night and hiding under the banks of the river during the day, they eluded the trailing Indians. Mrs. Chase had brought with her a loaf of bread which didn't last long. They had fish hooks and thread which they fashioned into fishing lines. Enough fish were caught to keep them from starving.

While hiding out during the day they could hear the Indians prowling about, so no travel was attempted. Travel at night was a nightmare as they stumbled and fell against sharp volcanic rocks which shredded their footwear and opened ugly wounds in their flesh. After they had traveled about 70 miles the men became too weak from hunger to carry the young children. The children would cry from hunger and pain. The adults would try to keep them quiet by cajolery or sometimes by force, for fear they would give away their

position to the searching Indians.

They crossed the Snake River again near old Ft. Boise (located near the present town of Parma, Idaho), which had been completely abandoned in 1854. After crossing the river, they were unable to find the trail again, so they camped on the Owyee River. There, they found and butchered a poor cow that had been abandoned by an earlier emigration party. The beef was supplemented with a few wild berries which provided nourishment a few more days.

While at the Owyee River camp, they found a camp on the Snake River occupied by friendly Indians. Some articles of clothing and ammunition were traded for salmon.

At that final camp on the Owyee were Alexis Vanorman, Mrs. Vanorman, Mark Vanorman, Mr. & Mrs. Chase, Daniel and Albert Chase, Elizabeth and Susan Trimble, Samuel Gleason, Charles and Henry Utter and an infant child of the murdered Mrs. Utter, George Myers, Mrs. Myers and five young children, Christopher Trimple, several children of Mrs. Chase and several of Mr. Vanorman.

It was decided they would try once again to send word of their plight to try and get help. Christopher Trimble, a boy of eleven, and an old man named Civilian G.

Present-day photo of the Owyhee River in Oregon, probably near the site of the emigrants' final camp.   Photo by Eugene E. Luckey

Munson were selected to go for help. They took whatever food could be spared and set out northward hoping to find the trail again. They found the trail and proceeded north-northwest until they reached Burnt River near the present town of Durkee, Oregon. On reaching that place they found the Reith brothers and Chaffey, one of the deserting soldiers.

Old man Munson went on with these men to Umatilla, Oregon, where they arrived on the 2nd of October. They reported the plight of the massacre survivors to Indian Agent Byron N. Davis. Mr. Davis immediately dispatched two men with a horse load of provisions to hasten to meet the survivors as soon as possible. At the same time a loaded wagon drawn by oxen was also sent out from the agency.

Young Trimble did not go on with the men to Umatilla. Instead, he returned to the emigrant camp from Burnt River to offer hope to the other survivors that help was on its way. He found they were still without sustenance but were keeping themselves alive with frogs they caught crawling along the river.

Out of a company of 54 persons, 39 lives had been lost, a large amount of property wasted, and indescribable suffering endured for six weeks.

During the next few days the local Indians made several visits to the emigrants' camp and traded food for guns and clothing. The clothing was sorely missed and the white people suffered much, as the nights were cold. But everyone was so hungry they could not resist any trade for food.

Alarmed lest the savages strip him of all his clothing and end by killing him, Vanorman set out to the north hoping to meet the relief party, if there was one. He was accompanied by his wife and five of his children, Samuel Gleason and Charles and Henry Utter. All their bodies were later found at Burnt River, murdered by savages.

The condition of the still-living in the emigrants' camp was becoming more and more critical. Deaths were occurring regularly and subsistence had become non-existent. Finally, the relief parties from the Indian Agency and Captain Dent with his 100 men reached the camp on the Owyee — 45 days after the initial wagon train attack on the Snake River. When the troops came into the camp of misery, they wept. They thought Capt. Dent was cruel to prevent them from scattering food among the half-naked living skeletons stretched upon the ground, but he knew too much food would make the starving people ill or possibly kill them. The Myers family, Mrs. Chase and one child, and Mr. Trimble were all who were alive at the camp.

Out of a company of 54 people, 39 lives had been lost, a large amount of property wasted, and indescribable suffering endured for six weeks.

When Capt. Dent arrived with the rescued survivors, the Blue Mountains were already covered with snow, which a little later, would have prevented his return to Umatilla. ∎

what he said: "that monument in Pioneer Park stating that immigrants crossed the river at that point is a disrespect to the pioneers. Why should the wagon trains pick that steep, rock-faced place to cross when just upstream there was an excellent ford?" "The ford," he said, "was about half way between the Sisemore place and the Staats place, in the vicinity of the mill pond."

You know, I think the old fellow was right. I went and looked at the Deschutes River in the vicinity of the Colorado Street bridge (just below the present mill pond) and it appears to be a *much* better place to ford than the Pioneer Park area!

However, there is another very serious problem with the bronze plaque. It tells us that the pioneers forded the Deschutes River at Bend's Pioneer Park and then continued westward. But, for *what* purpose would *any* wagon train have forded the Deschutes River at Bend? There was never any wagon trail to anywhere on the *west* side of the river in this locality! As Keith Clark told me, "occasional cattle drovers might have forded the river in the Bend area, searching for new pastures — but certainly *no* wagon trains."

The various descendants of the Clarks and Vandeverts still hold periodic reunions. Sometimes they meet at the old Vandevert homestead ranch just south of Sunriver. This family has many, many old stories to tell and retell — stories that have been passed down from generation to generation. They reflect the pioneer heritage of our community and our American West. There are stories, truly, of kinds of iron men and women we seldom encounter today.

But, as Jim Gardner, the archivist of the Clark/Vandevert records, told me, "The big problem in trying to sort out the actions of the Clark Massacre party is an almost total lack of written family records for the mid-1800s." I'm sure that Jim and I must share some mutual feeling that there is some kind of vacuum in our historical cognizance of what *really* happened in this important era of our Central Oregon history. We need more *written* data!

For better or for worse, as far as the historian is concerned, the longer the old stories are told, the more entrenched and embellished they become. It does sometimes appear that the verbal history passed along to our heirs is not always the same as that which logic and written records may later suggest. But does it not seem to you, sometime, that the history presented to us is usually part fact, part myth, part mystery, and often mixed together with a generous portion of romance that makes it all come together in acceptable human terms?

It is an article of faith within the Clark/Vandevert family history that the 1851 Clark party left the established Oregon Trail (most likely at Vale's Malheur River crossing) and crossed central Oregon on Meek's old tracks and stayed for awhile in Bend on the banks of the Deschutes. And from Bend, they somehow went northward until they connected with the Barlow Road and thence to the Willamette Valley.

However, some of the family members I've talked to try not to be too dogmatic about the traditional story, although they may be unwilling to accept a different version until further documents surface which might clarify the story. Surprisingly, there were also several Vandeverts who frankly disagreed with the old story.

On September 30, 1970, five years before his death, Claude Vandevert (son of William P. Vandevert) made a surprising statement to historian Keith Clark. He said, in effect, "I doubt very much that the Clark Massacre party of 1851 ever came to Bend. They went to The Dalles by means of the old traditional Oregon Trail." He added that he realized that all the rest of the Vandeverts believed the old story, but that he had a problem with it because he knew the difficulties involved in travel south or north or west from Bend in 1851.

On March 1, 1992, this author was discussing Vandevert family history with Ruth Vandevert Lane of Prineville, Oregon. This 92-year-old lady knows a lot about that family history, as she is a granddaughter of Joshua Jackson Vandevert and Grace Clark Vandevert. (Their son Charles was Ruth's father.) While talking to my wife and me, Ruth suddenly volunteered the following information:

"You know, " she said with a grin, "Grace Clark never did ever see Bend after that attack in Idaho. As far as I'm concerned, they went up the regular old Oregon Trail, and Grace even bought some horses at The Dalles." And then she added, " That plaque down in Bend is just not true."

And there you have it. I have summarized the facts and opinions on this fascinating segment of local history as best I could find them. It must be understood that one treads on long-standing family traditions only with great trepidation and, hopefully, with a great deal of respectful concern for the parties involved.

Hopefully, in the future, new data will become available which will settle this controversy once and for all. At this time, you, dear reader, must decide for yourself which version of the 1851 Clark journey seems the most plausible.

As for myself, the fascination of history such as this is in its diversity of opinion and its contentions and surprises. Without those challenging elements, I don't think the story would be much fun at all! ∎

ACKNOWLEDGEMENTS:
Many thanks are due Keith and Donna Clark at the Deschutes County Historical Society, and to Ruth Vandevert Lane. They have been most helpful in providing the author with information, advice, and comments on this article.

SUGGESTED FURTHER READING:
Bend in Central Oregon – Ray Hatton, 1978

Conversations with Bullwackers, Muleskinners, Etc. –
    Lockley/Helm/1981

"Cutoff Fever" – Leah Collins Menefee

Oregon Historical Quarterlies, December 1976 through
    Spring 1978 (especially the September 1977 issue)

East of the Cascades – Phil Brogan, 1964

Gold and Cattle Country – Herman Oliver & E.R. Jackman, 1961

A History of the Deschutes Country in Oregon –
    Deschutes County Historical Society, 1985

" *The Lost Wagon Train of Elijah Elliott*" – Don Burgderfer,
    Cascades East magazine, Fall & Winter issues, 1991

Oregon's Great Basin – Denzel & Nancy Ferguson, 1978

Pioneer Roads in Central Oregon – Nielsen, Newman & McCart, 1985

Sage Jumping From Bend To Burns

By Gary Meier

Loaded "auto-trucks," at Wall Street and Oregon Avenue in Bend. In 1913 the Bend-Burns road was the longest truck route in the United States.   Photo courtesy Gary Meier.

BEND

HORSE RIDGE

Millican

Brothers

HAMPTON BUTT

Hampton

LEFT: Nostalgic drivers can still travel portions of the old Bend-Burns highway. This 1987 view looks west toward Horse Ridge from the Millican area.

BELOW: Sometimes an autoist needed help from a passing wagon in the early days on the Bend-Burns road. Photos courtesy Gary Meier.

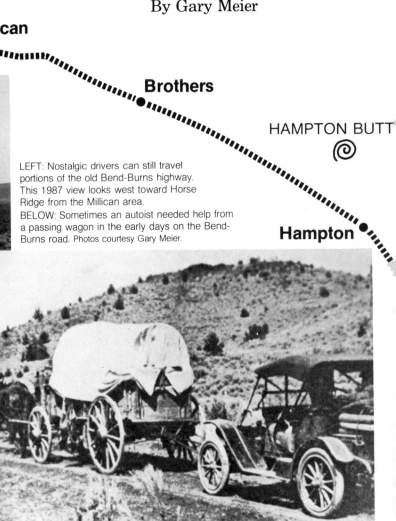

*Eleven hours after leaving Bend, May 7, 1911,
a group of tired, dusty "autoists" reached Burns
marking the official opening of the
150-mile Bend-Burns Road, now U.S. Highway 20.*

Thirty-five excited men held onto their hats with one hand and seats with the other as their seven big, open automobiles, decorated with ribbons and flags, bumped and bounced through the sage plains east of Bend on the morning of May 7, 1911. These adventurous "autoists" were members of the Bend Commercial Club and the occasion was a journey over the high desert to Burns, marking the official opening of the narrow, rough, 150-mile, sagebrush-dodging, sand track known as the Bend-Burns Road, now U.S. Highway 20.

The dusty group, tired but happy, was warmly received at Burns 11 hours after leaving Bend. Celebrations and speeches carried on into the night for, no matter how primitive, the long-awaited road from Bend was open. Travelers and freight would now have a straight through connection to the coming railhead at Bend. Passage to and from Bend, as well as Portland and other Oregon points, would be faster and cheaper than previous circuitous routes, opening the way for further development of the immense part of Oregon that pio-

neer cattleman Bill Hanley called "the big light country."

By February 1911, the call for a direct wagon and auto path from Bend to Burns had gained enough popularity at each end and with the many homesteaders in between, that Road Supervisor E. W. Richardson was sent out from Bend to survey the best route. He and his party, after spending a week on horseback viewing the country and

collecting data, reported that a road could be put in at minimal cost. The time to do so was at hand for the tracks of the Oregon Trunk Railway, part of James Hill's Great Northern system, were quickly being laid south to Bend.

In March a locating party, led by Richardson, trekked out across the high desert again to stake the actual course of the new road. Flags were stuck in the sand to mark the

The Bend to Burns Fast Freight and Express, circa 1913, prepares to head out over the high desert.
Photo courtesy Gary Meier.

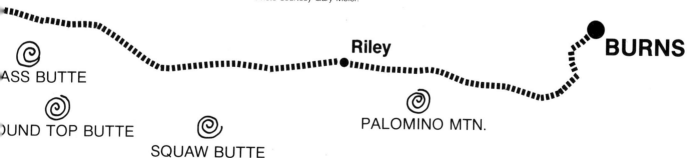

The desert cars that began making the rough trip to Burns were called "sage jumpers" and most of them were big, sturdy, powerful six- and seven-passenger automobiles.

The desert and the road required toughness and durability in a car, and many of the little lightweight city autos could not stand up to the rigors of what was soon generously called the Central Oregon Highway.

path for the building crew to follow. The road was to go around to the south of Horse Ridge and continue in an easterly and south-easterly 150-mile meander to Burns.

When he returned to Bend, Richardson announced that the desert settlers were so excited over the project that men, women, and children were already grubbing out sagebrush along the flagged route.

On March 27 Richardson led a crew of eight men, with 13 horses and a drag blade, to cut a 12-foot-wide swath. The heavy drag was pulled over the trail twice, removing much of the sagebrush. Another crew followed with grub hoes, picks, and powder to clear more brush and rocks. But no effort was made to lay a real bed. The roadway was to be merely a track over the natural surface.

Like most early roads of its kind, the first Bend to Burns road twisted, turned, and curved around countless rock formations, hills, and washes. The irregularity of the line was caused, too, by the necessity of skirting the property boundaries of many desert homestead claims.

After that initial May excursion by the Commercial Club came a time of adventurous motoring from Bend to Burns, for the early autos were obstinate and the primitive road was, as one old-timer put it, "dusty and doubtful." In those days the term "road" often meant simply a way through, and that aptly describes the first auto-path to Burns — a track across the desert.

Daring autoists began venturing out on the desert, leaving the green security of Bend with feelings of excitement mixed with fear. It was a long way to Burns, with few opportunities for aid or water should trouble arise.

When the railroad reached Bend in October 1911, the big lumbering eight-to-twelve horse freight wagons used the road, too, and many were the autos that became stuck in the sand when they pulled over to allow passage of a long horse-freight outfit. Wagon freighters, such as Joe Claypool, Tom Vickers,

and "High Pockets" Magoon, required ten days to haul between Burns and the railhead at Bend via the new road, a shorter time than the old way through Prineville.

The desert cars that began making the rough trip to Burns were called "sage jumpers" and most of them were big, sturdy, powerful six and seven-passenger automobiles. The desert and the road required toughness and durability in a car, and many of the little lightweight city autos could not stand up to the rigors of what was soon generously called the Central Oregon Highway.

Though many private vehicles were taken out on the Burns road, the majority of the desert cars were "for hire" auto stages. The usual fare was $20 for a round-trip ticket. And it was quite a trip.

Dallas Lore Sharp, an eastern professor, wrote this about his 1913 adventure from Bend to Burns:

"The clutch snapped in with a jump; forward, backward shot the lever — we were rounding a corner in a whirl of dust, Bend behind us, and the auto-stage like some giant jackrabbit bounding through the sagebrush for Burns, 150 miles across the desert." . . .

"I had never ridden from Bend to Burns by auto-stage before, and I did not realize at first that you could hold yourself down by merely anchoring your feet under the rail and gripping everything in sight. It is a simple matter of using all your hands and feet." . . .

"The desert was entirely new to me; so was the desert automobile. I had been looking forward eagerly to this first sight of the sage plains; but I had not expected the automobile, and could see nothing whatever of the sagebrush until I had learned to ride the car." . . .

"I thought I knew an automobile; but I found that I had never been on one of the Western desert breed. The best bucker at the Pendleton Round-up is but a rocking-horse in comparison. I doubt if you could experience death in any part of the world more times for 20 dollars than by auto-stage from Bend to Burns."

Though a wide variety of desert

cars were used on the Central Oregon Highway in the early days, several names stood out for their ruggedness and dependability. Among these stalwarts were big touring cars made by Buick and Packard. Garrett Coombs of Coombs' Auto Livery liked his 1913 seven-passenger Cadillac, and John Couch hauled people and freight in his large-model Reo.

Jackson "6s" were popular and the Portland dealer sold many to the desert area. The slogan of the Jackson Automobile Co. was "No Hill Too Steep — No Sand Too Deep."

Large air-cooled Franklins worked well in the high desert temperature extremes, but they were expensive: $4,000. Johnny Johnson operated a Franklin auto stage service to Burns and on some runs made the best time on the road, arriving only nine hours after leaving Bend.

The 1911 seven-passenger Nash Rambler Cross Country model performed well on the Bend to Burns road, too, and it boasted a new fea-

ture: a complete spare wheel came with the car, a decided advantage over carrying only a spare tire.

Claude Kelley drove a big Ford touring car between Bend and Burns for Blackwell's Auto-Stage Company. If the car was filled, he charged $10 per head.

The auto stage drivers carried a few necessities along with their passengers for the engines were balky and tires stuck easily in the sand, mud, and snow of the Central Oregon Highway. Tucked away or strapped on the cars were shovels, lanterns, tool boxes, spare parts, and traction devices such as Weed's Patented Chain Tire Grips. Extra gasoline was carried in five-gallon cans, and always the cars were equipped with spare cans of water.

In addition, tire repair items had to be carried, including Monkey Grip tire patches, hand pumps, tire tools, and a spare tire or two for those frequent occasions when razor-sharp lava rock would rip open a tire.

Much repair time was spent out on the desert by those wishing to go

from Bend to Burns, where services for autoists were scant. George Millican's place, 24 miles from Bend, was the first available stopping point for water, food, or gasoline. The tiny settlement of Brothers, 15 miles further east was not established until 1913, but after that time provided a waystop for autos.

The next welcome sight in the early years of the road, 1911 to 1915, was the tall Hampton Valley windmill at the homestead community of Imperial, 36 miles southeast of Millican. During the few years of the town's existence, there were two small stores, a garage, and, of course, a popular well. But soon, with failed crops and dead dreams, the homesteaders left Hampton Valley and Imperial was no more.

By far the most popular stopping place on the entire route was Brookings' Half Way House, located a few miles east of the Hampton settlement, on the south side of the road. The Brookings place, at Mile 72, was about halfway between Bend and Burns, and provided meals and lodging for travelers. It was a regular resting place for autoists, who could make Brookings in about six hours on a good day. It was also an overnight stopping point for the heavily loaded horse freighters, who reached the Half Way House in five days out of Bend or Burns.

In 1918 Bert Meeks bought the lodge and property and ran it until 1928. In that year, when the dirt roadway was improved by grading, Meeks opened the Hampton Station and Lunch Counter a few miles west and operated there until 1945.

The next available gas and water stop was 53 miles beyond Brookings at the Riley store. Riley was 25 miles from Burns and was also the first stop heading west.

Freight, as well as passengers, began being hauled by motor vehicles when the railroad reached Bend. On November 27, 1911, just one-and-a-half months after the golden spike ceremony in Bend, two big Packard "auto trucks," owned by the Central Oregon Trucking Co., left Bend for Burns. Each carried over 7,000 pounds of freight

Jess Tetherow (foreground) and his desert auto stage, c. 1912.   Photo courtesy Gary Meier

The early desert cars broke down frequently on the 150-mile, sagebrush-dodging track known as the Central Oregon Highway. Photo courtesy Gary Meier

bound for Harney Valley. It was a slow trip for the drivers, who spent the first night at Millican's and the second at Riley. They reached Burns on the third day, after 19 hours of actual driving time. The Packards used 50 gallons of gas going over, or the equivalent of one gallon for every three miles. The average speed was less than eight miles per hour.

Slow though the first trip was, it proved that large freight shipments could be hauled over the desert much faster than the ten days required by the horse-freight outfits. And from then until now, passenger cars began sharing the Central Oregon Highway with freight carriers.

On March 6, 1912, Mr. F. C. Riggs, Northwest Manager for the Packard Company, announced in the *Bend Bulletin* that the Bend to Burns road was the longest truck route in the United States and perhaps in the world.

Through the 1920s there were many changes in the Central Oregon Highway. Almost every year portions of it were relocated to follow a different course. In 1917 the Bend-Burns road was officially made part of the east-west U.S. Highway 20. But it still remained a simple, rough, dirt track over the desert, requiring autoists ten to fifteen hours to get from Bend to Burns, unless there was trouble on the way. Then it could take two or three days.

As late as 1926 the road conditions were not much improved. In an article titled "Over The High Desert," in the December 12, 1926 issue of the *Oregonian*, Automobile Editor Arthur Sullivan described an auto trip from Bend to Burns. "It is not much of a road, as roads go today," he wrote. "It is simply a trail — a one-way trail — across the desert."

Automobile Editor Sullivan particularly did not enjoy the return trip to Bend; he had two flat tires in the middle of the desert.

In 1930 a major realignment was made in U.S. Highway 20, including a route over Horse Ridge, 20 miles out of Bend. The highway was moved one-half mile north of Millican, and the entire length was paved. Between 1930 and 1963 several more shifts in the road location were made, particularly near Burns and over Horse Ridge, where the present route was cut through past the spectacular gorge of Dry River in 1963.

Portions of the old, original Bend to Burns road can still be seen. One of the best and longest stretches remaining can be found one-half mile south of Millican, where it crosses Pine Mountain Road. And for those not adverse to a dusty drive, the old road can be followed around the south edge of Horse Ridge, off Arnold Loop Road, all the way to the Millican airstrip. Arnold Loop Road itself was once a part of the Bend-Burns road.

U.S. Highway 20 still rides the high desert farther and more completely than any other major road in Oregon. The great rolling sage plains, scored by jagged rimrock cliffs and dotted with ancient, gnarled juniper trees, provides an inspiring change for town-dwellers hungry for the open spaces. Visitors to Oregon, too, are given the opportunity to see much of the wonderous variety of scenery in the state while traveling Highway 20 through Central Oregon.

Today travelers can whisk themselves to Burns or Bend in a little over two hours; leave Bend after breakfast and be in Burns before lunch. Long gone are the days when "autoists" ventured out in their "sage jumpers," never knowing if they would reach Burns in 11 hours or three days. ■

The Little Lava Lake MURDERS

Central Oregon's Own "Unsolved" Mystery

By Don Burgderfer

In December 1923, fur trappers Roy Wilson and Dewey Morris left their camp at Little Lava Lake and came home to Bend to spend the Christmas holidays. Before returning to the remote cabin on New Years Day, they told their friends and relatives they would probably return to Bend in February. However, this holiday visit was to be the last time their families would ever see them alive.

The two men were based at Ed Logan's cabin at Little Lava Lake. Ed was raising some rather valuable foxes for the fur trade and had hired Ed Nichols to stay at the cabin and care for the five animals. It was lonely out there in the wintertime and Nichols was glad to have Roy and Dewey for company. The two trappers helped Ed a bit with the foxes and also ran extensive trap lines for martin, fox and other fur-bearing animals.

On January 15, 1924, Allen Willcoxen was making his way through the snow on a periodic inspection trip to the Elk Lake Resort, which he owned. He stopped at the trappers' cabin at Little Lava and, since the hour was growing late, decided to spend the night there and continue on to Elk Lake the following day. The four men got little sleep as they sat up most of the night swapping tales and maybe taking a little nip of moonshine now and then. Willcoxen left the next morning, and he was the last person from Bend to see these men alive.

February came and passed, as did March and almost half of April. No one in Bend could figure out why the trappers had not returned. On April 13, two relatives set out to see what happened. One was H.D. Innes, a brother-in-law of Roy Wilson, and Owen Morris, brother of Dewey Morris. What they found when they arrived at the Little Lava Lake cabin was disturbing. An emaciated cat bolted out the door when it was opened. The breakfast table was set and food was on the stove. The calendar was still turned to January. Outdoor hats and coats were still in the cabin, and guns and traps did not appear to have been disturbed. But, the five valuable foxes were missing from their pens. This was ominous, indeed, and the men returned to Bend that evening.

On April 14, Pearl Lynes returned to the lake with Innes and Morris to help in the search, and on the 15th Donald and Ben Morris and Redmond sheriff deputy Clarence A. Adams joined the searchers. For some reason unknown, Sheriff Samuel E. ("Bert") Roberts declined to visit the scene. However, Adams was reputed to be quite familiar with the area and the men's trap lines.

It was known the trappers kept a food cache near the Crane Prairie Dam, and that there were three other cabins along the trap lines. But, no trace of the men was found at those places. Everyone wondered why experienced woodsmen would walk away from their cabin and leave coats, hats, guns and snowshoes behind. Any kind of tracking was out of the question because of the snow that had fallen since January. Pearl Lynes was now convinced that the men must have been lured out of the cabin

This was Ed Logan's cabin at Little Lava Lake. Searchers found no signs of violence inside the cabin, leading them to the conclusion that the trappers were lured outside to their deaths. The old cabin has long since disappeared from the area. Photo courtesy of Mary Fraser.

and killed in some unknown manner.

Then the trappers' tote sled was found partly submerged at the edge of (big) Lava Lake, three-fourths of a mile away. The sled had blood and hair on it, and a frozen-over hole was seen out in the lake ice. The searchers were now fairly certain they knew the location of the missing trappers.

Carcasses of the missing foxes were found near the cabin. All but one especially valuable silver fox had been inexpertly skinned out, with the feet simply cut off instead of being skinned out. This led to the belief that at least two different people were involved. The presence of uneaten food in the fox pens was proof enough to Ed Logan that strangers had been around and had upset the usually voracious but also easily upset foxes.

On April 23, while awaiting further developments, H.D. Innes and Deputy Adams hiked over to Lava Lake to catch some fish. They left Ed Logan at the Little Lava cabin to fix supper. The ice had rather rapidly come off the lake, and at 5:30 pm they noticed three

bodies floating about 200 yards from shore. They borrowed a nearby boat and brought the bodies near the shore and tied them there. The next day, more people came to help and the bodies were removed from the icy waters and brought to Bend.

It is known that Paul Hosmer was one of the party that brought the bodies out, and it is assumed that Paul, a well-known writer and photographer, took most of the photos of the recovery process that came into this author's hands.

At 2:30 pm the next day, April 25, 1924, the Reverend Beard held a funeral service for the men at the Methodist Church. Dewey Morris, age 24, was single and was the son of John and Hattie Morris. Edward Nichols, age 53, was the son of Thomas Nichols and was a widower. Harry Leroy ("Roy") Wilson, age 36, was single and was the son of Charles and Sarah Wilson. Roy was a veteran of the U.S. Marine Corps, 108th Company, 8th Regiment. The three comrades were laid to rest in adjoining grave sites at the Greenwood Cemetary.

Once the bodies of the trappers

had been examined, there was no question that the rankest of foul play had occurred at Little Lava Lake. And the observers were pretty confident that the killings took place out-of-doors, since the cabin betrayed no evidence of violence or struggle. As Pearl Lynes had suggested, the men were somehow lured outside, killed, tied up, hauled over to the larger Lava Lake on their own tote sled, and then shoved through a hole chopped in the ice. It was estimated this all happened on or a bit after January 15. Coroner C.P. Niswonger and Dr. R.W. Hendershott had done postmortems and decided the death instruments were a shotgun, a revolver and a hammer.

Roy Wilson had been the first body removed from the lake. He had been killed by a bullet to the head and had also been shotgunned. One shotgun blast had even torn away the point of his right shoulder.

Ed Nichols (spelled "Nickols" on his gravestone, in his father's manner) was still wearing his spectacles when recovered. He had been shotgunned.

Dewey Morris had been killed by blows on the head with a blunt instrument and had also been shotgunned. (A bloodstained hammer had been found outside the cabin earlier.)

What was the motive for such vicious mayhem? It had been rumored the three trappers had collected almost $3000 worth of furs, not to mention the foxes that Ed Logan had, valued up to $1800 by some reports. Those pelts may have seemed like motive enough, but there were others who thought that revenge was also a factor in the killings. Who would be so malevolent as to exact revenge this way? There was a ready-made suspect lurking out there, and his name was on everyone's lips. He had even been seen in the area earlier.

The Suspect

Enter now a character upon whom the ensuing manhunt focused almost totally, a person so despicable that no crime was beyond him, not even triple murder. His Idaho state pen portraits made the front page of the Bend *Bulletin* on April 24, 1924. His name was Charles Kimzey, though most people around Bend knew him as Lee Collins, one of many aliases he used in his travels throughout the west. Sheriff Roberts requested that the county court offer a $1000 reward for Kimzey (they later offered $750 and another $750 for Kimzey's accomplice.)

Kimzey was well known to Ed Logan. At a prior time he had done a bit of work for Ed, and then stole a valuable fur coat from Ed's home in Bend and shipped it to himself in Idaho. (It was recovered before Kimzey could pick it up.) Logan claimed that Kimzey wanted to "get" him and that he may have even thought that Ed was staying at his cabin when the slayings took place. Still, Logan was a bit puzzled. He definitely felt Kimzey was implicated, but somehow didn't feel the crime was quite Kimzey's style (whatever that meant).

The breakfast table was set and food was on the stove. The calendar was still turned to January. Outdoor hats and coats were still in the cabin, and guns and traps did not appear to have been disturbed. But, the five valuable foxes were missing from their pens.

Kimzey also was unhappy with all the trappers at the cabin because they had previously given information to authorities that had almost gotten him arrested in Idaho. He would have *enjoyed* getting even for that.

It was known that Ed Nichols, one of the murdered men, was in constant fear that Kimzey might show up again. He had a run-in with Kimzey the prior August and Kimzey had stolen $500 that Ed had been saving.

Prior to all this, on August 21, 1923, Kimzey had rented a cab to take him east of town. Near Last Chance Ranch (60 miles SE of Bend near the Deschutes-Lake County line) he struck the driver, James Harrison, with a pistol, tied his feet and hands, forced him to drink some poison and then dumped him in a dry well. He then stole the Jewett cab and took off for Idaho. But, Mr. Harrison did not die and was later found by line-riders! Though his hearing was somewhat impaired by the pistol-whipping, he did survive his ordeal.

Kimzey had a few other charges trailing after him. He was suspected of having some involvement in a murder in Chiloquin, and he had attempted to poison a Montana sheepherder he was unhappy with. The next year, in 1925, he allegedly murdered a Salt Lake City man, Mr. W.R. Howard, whose body was disposed of in the Nevada desert. Kimzey and Howard had left Salt Lake City together on December 7, 1925, in Howard's car, headed for California. It was alleged that Kimzey, using the alias "William Becker," later cashed traveller's checks belonging to Howard and also had in his possession other property of Howard's.

What was Charles Kimzey like? Ed Logan said that Kimzey was an escapee from the Idaho State Penitentiary. In fact, Kimzey had entered the Idaho pen on June 18, 1915, and escaped on October 11, 1915, when he still had 14 years to serve. For some odd reason, though, he was not considered a wanted man by Idaho prison authorities. Even stranger, after escaping the institution in Boise, he became a government trapper for three years — headquartered in Boise! In 1924 he was about 39 years old, 5'7" tall and about 160 pounds. He had worked as a sheepherder and shearer, a ranch hand, a trapper, and a teamster. He had a habit of talking rapidly through his teeth and one almost always saw his teeth when he talked. It was said he walked erectly, but with toes pointed out.

On April 22, just before the bodies of the victims surfaced, two Deschutes County deputies had been sent to Klamath Falls to investigate the sale of some fox pelts there. However, it was a false alarm and the furs were not Ed Logan's, as had been suspected. Then, something else turned up.

Kimzey's "man wanted" poster had been widely circulated. A Portland traffic policeman was positive that Kimzey was one of two men who had stopped him on a Portland street and asked for directions to a fur store. The men were carrying a gunny sack full of furs. The officer, W.C. Bender, gave the men directions to the Schumaker Fur Company and there, on January 22, 1924, one of the men talked to the president of the firm, Carl Schumaker. After a half-hour of bargaining, the man sold the furs

What was the motive for such vicious mayhem? It had been rumored that the three trappers had collected almost $3000 worth of furs. Those pelts may have seemed like motive enough, but there were others who thought that revenge was also a factor in the killings. Who would be so malevolent as to exact revenge this way?

for $110. Mr. Schumaker asked the "trapper" for identification for his records. He was then shown the trapper's license of murder victim Ed Nichols!

That was almost the end of the story. By the end of April, the Bend *Bulletin* hardly even mentioned the Lava Lake murders. Kimzey stayed out of sight and his whereabouts were unknown until 1932. In March of that year, under the name Tom Rose, he was arrested in Helena, Montana, for violation of national prohibition laws. Then, on July 10, 1932, he was arrested on a bad check charge in Great Falls, Montana. However, he was released from the county jail before word arrived from Oregon authorities as to his true identity. And Charles Kimzey vanished again!

On February 17, 1933, there was a report that Kimzey, using the alias Bob Bales, had been arrested in Kalispell, Montana, an area where it was suspected he might be hiding out. It was now nine years since the Little Lava Lake murders, but a new Deschutes County sheriff, Claude McCauley, had entered office in 1928 and was keeping the case alive.

Bob Bales steadfastly denied he was Kimzey, and he really didn't look much like the photos available. By February 20, Kimzey's fingerprints had arrived and they were not the same as Bales'. So Bales went free. But, the hunt for Kimzey in northwest Montana

continued. And it took a strange twist.

Captured and Tried

A Kalispell jailer had been reviewing Kimzey's photos in February as a result of the Bob Bales arrest. Almost a month later, he was walking down the street in Kalispell and spotted the same Charles Kimzey he had seen in those photographs! Deputies were quickly alerted and the arrest was made. The aging criminal was 47 years old now, was growing quite bald, and said he hadn't heard the name Kimzey in years. He did not deny his true identity.

Curiously, Kimzey had been completely unaware of the furor surrounding the earlier arrest of Bob Bales. And three different states wanted to extradite Kimzey from Montana: Oregon (3 murders, 1 attempted murder), Nevada (1 murder), and Idaho (prison escape, car theft, forgery, bad checks, burglary). Even the federal government wanted him for driving Mr. Howard's car across state lines during the commission of a felony.

The Deschutes County grand jury was quickly called into special session so that extradition could be supported by *their* indictments rather than just the earlier justice court warrants. They also wanted to get their hands on him before anyone else did. However, Charles Kimzey, thinking he was being indicted just for the Little Lava

Lake murders, figured he'd better get to Oregon fast and he *waived* extradition. You see, he had an alibi. And when he so readily admitted his identity to his captors, he also quickly volunteered the information, "They think I killed those trappers in Oregon, but I didn't. I was in Colorado working on the Moffatt Tunnel at the time."

On March 17, 1933, Charles Kimzey was returned to Bend by Sheriff Claude McCauley and state police Corporal Art Tuck. Meanwhile, Kimzey embellished his alibi by stating he had eaten Christmas dinner, 1923, at the Moffatt Tunnel. He even named contractors he had worked for and the hotel where he stayed at West Portal. Officials busied themselves trying to check out all this new information, but Kimzey had left his usual confusing trail of aliases. It now became clearer why Kimzey thought he'd be better off in Oregon than in Nevada, where his deadly mayhem might have been more easily proved.

On March 18, Kimzey was told about something he hadn't realized: he might also be indicted for the 1923 attempted murder of cab driver James Harrison. He was aghast to learn Harrison was still alive, living in California, and quite willing and able to testify!

The first part of April, Kimzey was taken to Portland so officer Bender and Carl Schumacker could pick him out of a lineup. However, much to the consternation of authorities, neither man could make an absolutely positive identification of Kimzey as being one of the men with the bag of furs.

The Deschutes County grand jury was selected on April 10 and started taking testimony immediately.

No. 62

The Little Lava Lake
MURDERS

Central Oregon's Own "Unsolved" Mystery

By Don Burgderfer

PART II

Time has removed from us most of the participants in this grim episode of Central Oregon history that occurred years ago. Kimzey, were he alive today, would be over 100 years old. As always, he would steadfastly deny through his teeth that he had anything to do with the Little Lava Lake murders of 1924. To this date, no person has ever been officially charged or tried for that unsolved crime. Most likely, no one ever will be.

State police Corporal Art Tuck, who had done a lot of investigation into the Lava Lake murders, was the first witness. On April 12, Kimzey was indicted — not for the Lava Lake murders — but for the Harrison escapade: "Assault and robbery while armed with a dangerous weapon." Bert Boylan was the prosecuting District Attorney and Ross Farnham was appointed defense attorney. A plea of "not guilty" was entered and the trial was scheduled for April 20 before Circuit Judge T.E.J. Duffy.

On the 20th, at least 150 people had crowded into the courtroom to watch the trial of the infamous criminal. In fact, there were so many people that some of the people in front had to be moved out to make room for jurors! James Harrison had been brought up from California for the trial and he made a positive identification of Kimzey as his assailant. Continual questioning by defense lawyer Farnham could not shake his story. On April 22, Kimzey was found guilty as charged, and sentencing was scheduled for April 25.

Judge Duffy had been made well aware of Kimzey's life of criminal depravation by the prosecuting attorney. He was of no mind to turn this sociopath loose on society again. In the judge's view, Kimzey had made five different attempts to kill Harrison: (1) threatening with a gun, (2) hitting on the head with a gun, (3) tying his feet and hands together, (4) administering a dose of poison, and (5) throwing him into the abandoned cistern.

During the sentencing hearing Kimzey had little to say. He did state he had relatives in Idaho and Oregon and he was 47 years old. For the most part, he just sat poker-faced through the whole thing, even when he was sentenced to life imprisonment at the Oregon State Penitentiary.

The next day, Charles Kimzey was transported to Salem to begin his term of imprisonment. Not for the three murders everyone said he committed, but for a botched affair that left the victim alive and able to testify. In order to be admitted to the state pen, he had been given an examination and a certificate of health by Dr. R.W. Hendershott —

On April 24, 1924, the recovered bodies were wrapped in canvas and trucked back to Bend for a more complete examination by Coroner Niswonger and Dr. Hendershott. Funeral services were held the next day. Photo courtesy of Mary Fraser.

the same doctor that had signed the death certificate of the three Little Lava Lake victims.

Still Many Questions

We are left with a lot of interesting questions regarding this case. Foremost, of course, is: Did Kimzey and an unknown accomplice really kill those trappers? What were the results of inquiries about Kimzey's Colorado alibis? Records still available at the Deschutes County Sheriff and District Attorney offices simply do not go back that far, according to their officials.

When Sheriff McCauley brought Kimzey back from Montana, he had given hints to the media he knew who Kimzey's accomplice was. Was he just blowing smoke? Nothing else was ever said, and that shadowy partner was never identified. Who was he? Was McCauley just trying to attract media attention?

It appeared that, one of the killed trappers, Ed Logan (and perhaps others) knew something of Kimzey's background, even that he was a prison escapee. In which case, how come nobody ever blew the whistle on this criminal? Were they afraid

of his vengeance (perhaps rightly so, in view of his violent nature)? And why did Idaho prison authorities not classify Kimzey as a wanted man after his escape from them?

Many in the community wondered about the actions of Sheriff S.E. Roberts when he first heard about the possibility that Morris, Wilson and Nichols had been murdered. He simply would not go to the scene. One source told me Deputy Adams became so emotionally disturbed after the bodies were retrieved that he had to be taken home that day by Mr. Innes. Then, a year later, Adams committed suicide. Community gossips alleged a possible bootlegging tie-in between the trappers and the sheriff's office, complete with payoff money to keep things quiet. But, I found no reports of stills in the Lava Lake area.

Time has removed from us most of the participants in this grim episode of Central Oregon history that occurred 66 years ago. Kimzey, were he alive today, would be about 105 years old. As always, he would steadfastly deny through his teeth that he had anything to do with the Little Lava Lake murders of 1924. To this

date, no person has ever been officially charged or tried for that unsolved crime. Most likely, no one ever will be.

And you and I can only wonder about what really happened at that lonely place on a cold and terrible day in January.

*   *   *   *

EPILOGUE: I stated earlier that the specific location of Kimzey was unknown from 1924 to 1932. An amazing piece of correspondence that just crossed my desk has put the lie to that. On June 5, 1928, C.E. Love, an investigator for the William Burns Detective Agency, wrote a report to his headquarters in Salt Lake City. That report was forwarded several days later to the Warden of the Idaho State Penitentiary with the comment that the information therein was "unusual in character." And it certainly *was* unusual.

It seemed the Burns operative was in Boise on other agency business and had been talking with the Captain of the Boise Police Department. He was told that just two weeks before, a murdered man's body had been found floating on a small lake just west of Boise. Most people in the community suspected the murderer was one Charles Kimzey, who lived with two brothers on the far side of the lake! Mr. Love was clearly puzzled as to why this well-known criminal had not been taken into custody by the authorities.

The Police Captain explained that the only directly accessible way to Kimzey's house was by boat, and that he and his brothers would hold people at bay with rifles until they ascertained their business. The brothers also kept eight or ten large dogs which alerted them to intruders who might be approaching from across or around the lake.

The Captain noted that Kimzey had such a notorious reputation as a "bad man" that he was simply unable to assemble a posse willing to tackle the job. And so, because of his fearsome reputation, he was pretty much left alone while ensconced in his lakeside fortress. He had even summoned a dentist recently to have all his teeth pulled (the dentist was then threatened and told to "say nothing"). Apparently, the warden who received this report from Burns wasn't anymore anxious to confront his escapee than the Captain was!

Charles Kimzey had an Oregon Parole Board hearing on June 11, 1942. He still wouldn't admit guilt in the Harrison affair and the prison psychiatrist gave a very poor prognosis for Kimzey's future should he be released. He was denied parole and his incarceration continued indefinitely. However, on August 4, 1945, (two days before the atomic bomb was dropped on Hiroshima) Kimzey escaped from the Oregon State Prison, but was returned there on August 10.

On August 5, 1957, at the age of 72, Charles Kimzey was paroled from the Oregon State Prison. And for us, the trail of our leading suspect ends here.

WANTED FOR MURDER
$1500 REWARD

$750 each for Charles Kimzey, alias Lee Collins, and his partner (unknown). The reward of $750 applies to any person arrested and convicted of the murder of three trappers at Lava lake, Deschutes County, Oregon, in January, 1924.

Charles Kimzey, ex-Idaho state penitentiary, No. 2316

DESCRIPTION

Height, 5 feet, 7 inches, weight 160 pounds, eyes blue; age, 38 years. Occupation, ranch hand, teamster, sheepherder, sheep shearer. Scars as follows: Scar on nose; scar on right cheek; scar on right wrist; scar on left shin. Dark spot back of left side. May be wearing heavy, sandy mustache.

Finger print classification }1 R 00 11; }1 R 00.

Kimzey talks rapidly, with teeth partly closed, and at the same time smiles, showing teeth. Is fast with a revolver, which is a .38 Colt's Special.

Photograph taken of Kimzey about 8 years ago. Face is now fuller, and hair much thinner on top than cut shows.

Kimzey and partner should be arrested on sight, and held incommunicado.

Brother officers, take no chances with these men, for they are desperate criminals, having killed three trappers at their cabin, without giving them a chance for their lives.

Unidentified man wore khaki suit, beaver hat, leather puttees. Weight 150 pounds, sandy complexion. Armed with .32 Colt's automatic, with two chips out of lower left handle, underneath.

Arrest and wire
S. E. ROBERTS, SHERIFF
Bend, Oregon
Bend, Oregon, May 7, 1924.

ACKNOWLEDGEMENTS I am much indebted to the staffs of the Deschutes County Historical Society, the Niswonger-Reynolds Funeral Home, the Oregon State Penitentiary and the Idaho Department of Corrections. And a special thanks to Mary Fraser for photographs and materials used in this story. Mary wrote an unpublished account of this episode in 1953, with the help of Phil Brogan of the Bend Bulletin newspaper. I'm not certain, but the photographs were probably taken by Paul Hosmer and provided by him to Phil Brogan, who later gave them to Mary.

The Great American
DIAMOND HOAX

A scam pulled off by a man from Central Oregon

By Robert W. Pelton

The dusty boots of two typical desert rats scuffed the mirror-like floor of San Francisco's Bank of California. They appeared to be prospectors, their faces shadowed by a heavy growth of ragged beard and burned by the wind and sun. Both men looked weary. Only their eyes, bright and sharp, betrayed their excitement as each placed a small deerskin bag on Arthur Wrenn's counter.

"We'd like to have these stones put in your safe for a few days," the taller of the two men said to the teller.

"Stones? What kind of stones?" queried Wrenn cautiously. During the 1870s, San Francisco banks readily accommodated prospectors who wanted to safely store their gold dust. But this particular request was unique.

"Diamond stones," John Slack, the tallest prospector responded quickly. "Here, take a look."

Arthur Wrenn carefully opened each bag and looked inside. He let out a quiet whistle as he peered at two impressive piles of diamonds. Then he asked, "Whose name should I put on the receipt?"

"John Slack," said the taller man. "You'd better put down my partner's name too — Philip

Arnold. We're going to go and pick up some grub and supplies, then get some sleep. We'll come for the stones tomorrow."

Wrenn could hardly conceal his building excitement, but he asked with elaborate carelessness, "Are you going back to dig for more of these?"

"Yeah," said Slack casually, "we're going back soon." And with that Slack and Arnold walked out of the bank.

Wrenn nervously waited until the men were out of sight and he ran back to the safe. His hands trembled as he let the stones pour through his fingers. Then he saw something he hadn't noticed previously. There were also numerous rubies and sapphires among the diamonds. In all, he quickly estimated that the stones must be worth at least $100,000 — and these were just the initial specimens! The raunchy desert rats undoubtedly had discovered a mine worth millions of dollars!

Wrenn then ran to the office of William C. Ralston, the bank president, and a leading San Francisco financier. He was more than a little skeptical: "A diamond mine in the West! You must be insane, Wrenn! That's impossible!"

Wrenn was insistent. He poured the glittering stones on Ralston's

desk and said, "See for yourself, Mr. Ralston, see for yourself."

"God! It's probably the biggest strike that ever occurred in America," cried Ralston as he saw the stones. "This will even dwarf the Comstock Lode!"

Slack and Arnold came in for their stones the next day. Wrenn greeted them and said, "Before I give you the bags of stones gentlemen, Mr. Ralston, our president, would like to talk to you. There's nothing wrong gentlemen, but this would be much to your advantage."

The prospectors eyed Wrenn suspiciously. They looked at each other with doubt, but at that moment, Ralston strode over and introduced himself. Assuming the two men were ignorant miners, he condescendingly escorted them to his inner office and gave them brandy and cigars. In a few minutes, two other banker friends, George D. Roberts and William M. Lent, dropped in and were quickly introduced. The reason for the gathering? Ralston felt that Slack and Arnold had discovered a fantastically rich diamond field — a treasure of such magnitude that it could not possibly be handled like any other gold or silver mine. There were too many far-reaching business consequences: world dia-

*In all,
he quickly estimated
that the stones
must be worth
at least $100,000 —
and these were just
the initial specimens!*

**The raunchy desert rats
undoubtedly had
discovered a mine
worth millions of dollars!**

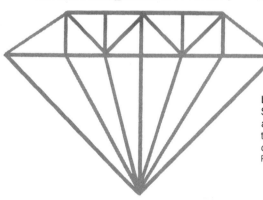

LEFT: Philip Arnold never lived to enjoy the $550,000 hidden in his safe. He died in a duel with a Prineville banker. RIGHT: John Slack, one of the two ragged prospectors who caused the furor of excitement over a nonexistent diamond mine. Photos courtesy of Robert W. Pelton.

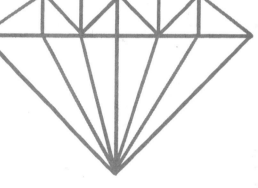

mond prices would be influenced; San Francisco just might become the world's diamond capital.

Slack and Arnold listened blankly. Then Slack spoke: "Guess you're right, Mr. Ralston. Arnold and me are willing to sell out for $660,000, right now! But you needn't worry about paying us yet. Just keep our stones in your bank and give us a couple thousand expense money. We'll go right on back to the mine and bring out a million dollars worth of stones for you and your partners."

Everyone agreed on the fairness of the offer and they gave Slack and Arnold the cash. But Ralston wasn't a fool. He hired private detectives to investigate the men's past. It was found that they were, indeed, prospectors, and had been for many years.

Ralton and his associates decided to form a ten-million dollar cor-poration to handle this stupendous new venture. Asbury Harpending, mining expert and financier, was brought in from London to act as their general manager. News of the diamond strike leaked out and the bank was soon besieged by people who wanted to invest. They were turned down. A newspaper editorialized: "Ralston, Lent, and Roberts have hold of a remarkable source of wealth and refuse to let their fellow citizens share it."

News of the bonanza swept the nation and leaped the Atlantic. Financiers in New York and Chicago tried to invest but were refused. Baron Rothschild contacted Harpending about joining the enterprise. Harpending, cautious and conservative, suggested that it might all be a hoax. Said Rothschild: "Don't be too sure of that. America is a large country. It has furnished the world with many surprises already. Perhaps it has others in store."

Arnold and Slack later returned to San Francisco and marched right into Ralston's office. Arnold toted a large buckskin bag over his right shoulder while Slack stood watchfully beside him, armed with a rifle and a revolver. Arnold opened the bag and poured out a provision of sparkling gems. "About a million dollars worth, I reckon," said Slack proudly.

Then Slack told his story. He said they had stumbled upon a rich part of the diggings and had gotten an estimated two million dollars worth of stones. These were placed in two bags, the largest of which was lost while crossing a flooded river on a raft. But they hoped that the bag brought in would suffice to prove their good intent.

Two lapidaries were called in to

inspect the stones. It was agreed that all were genuine. Then Ralston and his partners began to calculate. With 20 workers, a minimum of a million dollars in stones could be mined every month. Only one step remained to be taken before the deal could be closed. A mining expert would have to be allowed to check the diggings, and the location of the mining area would have to be disclosed to the bankers.

Investers Inspect the Diggings

Slack and Arnold agreed this was only fair. Henry Janin, a New York mining consultant, was brought in. Janin, Slack, Arnold, Harpending, and General George S. Dodge, an investor friend of Ralston's, formed the expedition to inspect the mine. They secretly journeyed to Rawlins, Wyoming, and bought horses. Then the men rode for four long days toward the Granite Mountains. As they approached the diamond field, Arnold pointed to a 40-acre area dotted with hills of dirt. "This is where we've dug our stones. All around this here place."

Harpending was the first to locate a diamond, laying in plain sight aside one of the dirt mounds. Janin was the next to find a gem. The men shouted at each other in excitement, and during the vocal exchange, Harpending thought he heard a distant train whistle. Gems by the score were quickly unearthed throughout the 40 acres. Occasionally a sapphire or a ruby was dug up. In two short days the happy expedition party had a large hatful of jewels. Janin was exhuberant and yelled, "There's no reason to dig any more. What must now be determined is the extent of the field, its accessibility to the railroad, and other technical details."

Arnold then spoke up: "I don't know about them there other things, but we're only about 90 miles from the railroad."

That simple statement reawak-

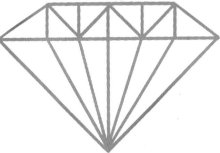

William C. Ralston, president of the Bank of California, was shattered, both physically and financially, by the hoax.
Photo courtesy of Robert W. Pelton.

ened Harpending's dormant suspicions. "You can't hear a train whistle 90 miles away," he whispered to Janin. "They must have led us here by a circuitous route. We're probably no more than 20 miles from the railroad. Why are they lying about that?"

He couldn't answer his own question, nor could he forget about it, even though Janin ignored what he said about the train whistle. Janin was too enthusiastic and his report coupled with the jewels uncovered was certain to make the deal go through as planned. And so it did when the party excitedly returned to San Francisco!

Ralston and his associates were convinced that the mining area would yield greater wealth than any other discovery made in America. They immediately bought out Slack and Arnold for the agreed upon sum of $660,000. The grandiose Diamond Company was formed and 25 prominent San Franciscans were allowed to invest $80,000 each in stock. Plans were made to import Amsterdam's best gem cutters to the city. Among the investors now was A. Gansl, a representative of the Rothschild family.

Suspicions Aroused

But Harpending was still very suspicious. He quietly hired Clarence King, a geologist-engineer, and dispatched him to the digging site. King and his helper, Wilhem Berry, were told to look in an area about 20 miles from the railroad. And that was where they found the so-called mine. Both men dug up gem after gem and King was also convinced the field was no doubt the greatest of the world's mineral discoveries. But then Berry, however, who had continued digging, stooped to pick up another diamond. He noticed that it bore the mark of a lapidary's tool.

"Look here, Mr. King," was his astonished remark. "This here is the bulliest diamond field as never was. It not only produces gems but cuts them also!"

King grabbed for the diamond. "Salted!" he gasped.

Then and only then did the entire hoax become clear. Hundreds of jewels had been planted in the earth. Then the gems had been left for a year to allow the rain and snow to "weather" the mine and make it appear to be natural.

Meanwhile, in San Francisco, the excitement was ever mounting. Many other mining firms were bidding hundreds of thousands of dollars for leases to adjoining lands. World famous jewelry companies were offering huge sums for the concession to cut and market the finished jewels. Then, a simple three-word telegram from King to Harpending burst the incredible bubble! It read: "SALTED: CLARENCE KING."

Bank president Ralston was stunned and near collapse. He ordered all investors be given back their invested cash and publicly admitted he had been duped. Bank of California business affairs were in complete disarray and a board meeting was called. Ralston was barred from the meeting. He left for home a dejected, haggard man, and went for a private swim at nearby North Beach. His body was later found in the water — whether he committed suicide or died of a

Continued on page 40

PERILOUS JOURNEY
A Crater Lake Expedition of 1874

*A fascinating account of the struggle to lower an intact boat
from the rim of Crater Lake and embark
on an expedition to Wizard Island*

By Lucile McKenzie

On August 16, 1874, a small boat sat poised on the rim of Crater Lake approximately 1,100 feet above the water. The young men and women clustered around it contemplated the almost perpendicular drop of the slope with apprehension and wondered how to get the boat and themselves down to the lake intact.

It had already been an arduous journey, many weeks in planning. John Kuykendall and his son, William, had built a "good boat, a small but sturdy craft," and set their departure date. Other members of the group were Henry Kuykendall, Charles S. Moore, his sister Frankie, Lessie Kuykendall, Kate Pearson, William Watson and son Eddy, Herbert Dyar, and E.W.

View of Wizard Island from the west rim of Crater Lake taken in August, 1874, the same month and year of the Agency Expedition. Photo by Peter Britt, courtesy of University of Oregon, Oregon Collection.

Hammond. Most of them were Government employees of the Klamath Indian Agency at Fort Klamath.

The planned trip was a daring venture. In 1874 Crater Lake was still something of a mystery. Only 21 years earlier John Wesley Hillman became the first white man to discover it when he led a party of prospectors through the area. No one knew how deep it was, and although visited often, only twice before had anyone actually been out on the water. The Agency employees hoped to lower an intact boat down to the lake surface and make a scientific/exploratory trip to Wizard Island. Along the way they would take soundings to determine the lake's depth.

The trip was not easy. There were no roads or trails after leaving the old Rogue River Route. Transportation was by horse and wagon, and the trip would take two days.

On the second day they left the road and wound their way up the trackless slopes toward the rim of the lake. E.W. Hammond recalled,

"We crossed a gully with a rollicking stream singing along its rocky bed. Then we moved to the right, again wound about among the fallen timber, crossed another rivelet, then up the slope, turning to the left ... over and around the logs up the hill and into the heavy timber, after which we failed to keep an account of our many windings and turnings."

As they approached the lake from the southwest, Hammond, who was most familiar with geological formations, attempted to find a suitable place to lower the boat, while the rest of the party set up camp. He began his survey of the treacherous terrain along the top of the rim, which varied in height from 500 to 2,000 feet above the lake. Climbing over the steep, rocky slope, he despaired of finding an appropriate spot. Nowhere along the water's edge was there anything that could be called a beach, a circumstance which complicated Hammond's task.

Eventually, however, he found a couloir, a deep mountainside gully

filled with debris, boulders and huge rocks. Although the spot was about 1,100 feet above the water, Hammond believed it would be safer to lower the boat down a couloir than from the tip of a ridge. Other places along the rim were lower, but generally were very steep, filled with loose, gravelly material, with no place to attach a rope. The couloir Hammond selected had a bank of late snow over which the boat could be lowered. Pleased with his choice, he climbed toward the top. As he neared the edge of the couloir, he glanced back down and nearly canceled the trip. The slope of the escarpment looked so terrifying that the task ahead seemed impossible. Swallowing his fear, Hammond forced himself to climb back down and re-check several huge boulders to ascertain they were firmly embedded in the earth. These boulders would be needed for support and they could not afford to have one come loose. Satisfied, Hammond joined his companions and they decided to lower the boat

A present day view of Wizard Island taken from a similar vantage point as the photo on the left.
Photo by A. Dean McKenzie.

the next morning.

They had brought along every bit of rope they could find and these pieces were tightly knotted together. As the boat teetered on the edge of the snowbank, the young women, to the annoyance of William Kuykendall, grew frightened and declared that, "It is impossible," "The sides are too steep," "It's totally impractical," and "Everyone will be killed."

In spite of these dire predictions, the ropes were tied securely, one end around the boat, the other around a spruce tree. Herbert Dyar, William Kuykendall, and Charles Moore volunteered to go down the slope with the boat. The rope was carefully let out by Hammond while the three men slipped and slid alongside the boat in a desperate attempt to keep it from plunging down the slope on its own.

When the rope was let out, the boat was secured in place and Hammond, John and Henry Kuykendall, inched their way down to the boat and to their three companions, picking up the rope as they went. The process was repeated with extreme care. One of the more pressing dangers was that the men approaching the boat from above might inadvertently start a landslide of rocks down upon the men holding the boat. Eventually this possibility became so real they had to abandon the rope-lowering method. They threw the rope in the boat and, holding it three men to each side, they relied on the combined strength of the six of them to hold it steady.

Hammond recalled, "Our progress down the slope was not as steady as might be desired. Sometimes we went faster than providence would dictate. Several times boat, rocks and all hands went sliding down together." They were very frightened, faced with the real possibility they would all plunge down onto the rocks at the lake's edge. Hammond said, "Two or three times I was under the boat with everything about me sliding at an alarming rate down the steep incline."

A present day view of a western crater slope seen from a boat on Crater Lake. This slope would probably be similar to those encountered by the expedition party in 1874. Photo by A. Dean McKenzie.

A little over halfway down they came to a long, sheer strip of snow down which the boat would have to pass, and they knew that here the boat must again be lowered by ropes. The ropes were re-attached to the boulders and the lowering process resumed.

Suddenly Herbert Dyar lost his footing on the snow and slid with terrifying speed toward the rocks below, while his companions stood frozen with horror. Desperately he grabbed at rocks, bushes and anything in his reach, and broke his descent just before he would have smashed onto the rocks. He later commented he was convinced that never in his life had he traveled so fast.

Shaken, they continued lowering the boat with the ropes and at last reached the rocks at the edge of the lake where they removed the sliding boards nailed to the bottom of the boat to protect it from rocks. Finally they set it in the water.

Historically this was the first time an intact boat had been lowered from the lake rim. Both times before when boats had been on the surface of Crater Lake, they were carried down in sections and built on the lake's edge. Now, four of the party jumped in the boat and rowed a short distance away from the shore so those on top would know they were safe. The boat leaked a little from the removal of its sliding boards but otherwise seemed safe. They tied it securely and began the climb to the top. Going up was easier than going down. They made it to the top in a remarkable 39 minutes. It had taken a tense hour to get down.

The next morning they prepared for the trip to Wizard Island.

Frankie Moore, Lessie Kuykendall and Kate Pearson overcame their fear and decided to go along, even though they were apprehensive about the climb down. They were excited at being the first women on the lake. Hammond noted that once before Miss Hannah Rolls of Jackson County had been to the lake's edge, but not out on the water.

After a cautious, but relatively uneventful climb down, the leaks were repaired with pitch and William Kuykendall gave the women a short boat ride to calm their nerves. It was an incredible experience for these young women. They were awestruck at the dramatic splendor of the cliffs that towered above them, while below lay water of unfathomed depth. It was a sobering moment, but the adventure appealed to them and they pronounced themselves ready for the trip to the Island.

Two trips were necessary to get everyone over to the Island. Since each trip took about 25 minutes one way, it was nearly noon when they began the climb to the summit. On top they found wild flowers blooming, and a small growth of trees that covered a narrow rim surrounding a crater Hammond described as "shaped like a pressed wash pan." Many of the trees around Wizard Island's rim have since died and stand like ghostly reminders of this day over a hundred years ago.

They had a picnic lunch inside the crater and put a bottle with their names in it among the rocks on the southwest rim. Later, William Kuykendall, Moore and Hammond took the women back to the mainland while the others stayed behind to measure the height and diameter of the rim.

As Hammond and Kuykendall rowed back across the lake to Wizard Island they encountered a series of strong squalls that threatened to capsize the small boat. Hammond said, "So light was the boat with only two of us in it that I found it fully as much as I could do to keep the boat from paying off before the wind when struck by one

of the squalls that by now had become quite frequent." Relieved, they tied up on the shore of Wizard Island and picked up the remaining members of the party.

But their work was not finished. They hoped to find the as yet unknown depth of Crater Lake. They knew that the Fay and Duskin party in 1869 failed to find the bottom with a 700 foot line. Comparing Crater Lake to other volcanic lakes, they decided the depth must be at least 2,000 feet. Therefore, they had a line 2,700 feet long, marked off at 50 and 100 foot intervals, wound up on a reel. They planned to make soundings between Wizard Island and the main shore. Halfway to the mainland, fighting the wind, they tossed the line out where they thought the greatest depth would be. But the line only went down 220 feet, a depth Hammond deemed, "Ridiculous for a lake which is supposed to be almost bottomless." Another spot yielded about 675 feet, but the last sounding gave only 200 feet. The measurements were inconclusive and for the time being Crater Lake's depth remained a mystery. The bottom eventually was found at 1,932 feet, which made the Agency employees' estimate off by a mere 68 feet.

When they reached shore, they tied the boat securely to leave it for anyone who might come later. William Kuykendall lamented, "It seemed a shame to leave this boat which served us so well, to be crushed by the snow and ice of the following winter."

Crater Lake's shimmering beauty made a lasting impression on the minds of those who embarked on this historic venture. Hammond marveled, "Were the lake narrow, or of some small extant, with such an escarpment, it would be grand indeed, but it would be terrible. Its contemplation would impress the mind with a sense of power, mighty it is true, but painful and oppressive." He added, "As it is, it is perhaps the most magnificent sheet of water in the world." A century later, we would firmly agree. ■

heart attack, no one knows.

Harpending was furious and initiated a search to locate Slack and Arnold. He also launched another investigation and soon found a London gem dealer who revealed important information. It seems that two years previously, Arnold had come into his office and asked to look at some undergrade African diamonds. Fifteen thousand dollars worth of the gems had been purchased as well as $2,000 worth of low-grade rubies and sapphires.

Only $17,000 worth of inferior jewels had been utilized to salt a 40-acre tract — a worthless piece of land that had stirred financial circles on two continents; brought forth millions of dollars in investments; brought about the untimely death of a bank president; and contributed to the closing of the Bank of California. And this same piece of land yielded Slack and Arnold — two simple desert rats — $660,000 in cash!

John Slack simply disappeared and was never heard from again. Arnold was finally traced to the place where he grew up — Prineville, Oregon. Harpending demanded the return of the $660,000, but Arnold refused. He emphatically denied salting the mine, and admitted he had $550,000 in his safe — money he claimed to have made from prospecting over the years. Pressed by Harpending, he finally but grudgingly handed over $150,000. So far as Arnold was concerned, the whole diamond mine affair was forgotten. He refused to even discuss the situation.

Philip Arnold's troubles were not yet over. He became involved in a bitter feud with a local Prineville banker and was challenged to a duel. Both men, armed with shotguns, met on the main street of town. The incensed banker fired first. Arnold was blown apart and died where he fell. With him also died the full disclosure of the fantastic diamond hoax. It remains today as probably the greatest and most skillfully concocted jewel scam in mining history. ■

Central Oregon's Best Known Building

A lively and controversial history surrounded the construction of the Crook County Courthouse in Prineville.

By David Braly

Front view of the Crook County Courthouse photographed over 50 years ago before the side entrance stairs, trees, and fence were removed. Photo courtesy of the Crook County Historical Society.

Central Oregon. To visitors, those two words conjure up visions of mountains, forests, deserts, sun, and snow. Products of nature. But there's one attraction here that was the product of an English fancy cake decorator who arrived in Prineville on a bicycle in 1897. It, along with old sawmills and the bridge over the Crooked River Gorge and a few other things, is one of this region's rare human-made attractions.

Seats of governments are often attractions. County courthouses only occasionally qualify. The Crook County Courthouse in Prineville would barely be noticed in a big, old Eastern city. In the Oregon outback, however, it is something special. No other building in Central Oregon is as quickly recognized or as well known as this three-story stone structure that sits snugly in the center of the Ochoco Valley. Its tall clock tower commands a panoramic view of that valley, and the clock tower can be seen for miles.

Jack Shipp built it. A native of England, Shipp had become a baker, and later a bicycle repairman, house builder, lumber executive, and civic leader. He also played cornet in the local band. In addition to the courthouse, Shipp built two churches and several

large houses — mansions by early Central Oregon standards. One was the Baldwin house, which is on the National Register of Historic Places. Shipp and his subcontractors took over the courthouse job after the project had become mired by years of controversy.

At the turn of the century, Crook County was Central Oregon and Central Oregon was Crook County. Deschutes and Jefferson counties didn't exist. The areas now occupied by those two counties were back then part of Crook. People in the western region of Crook — in

the area that now forms Deschutes and Jefferson counties — believed that the county's government favored the eastern section, and they also got the short end of county services. West county residents were especially irritated that roads in their section were so bad while their tax dollars went to projects that benefited the east side of the county.

Thus it came as a shock to west side residents when they learned of a secret plan by the Crook County Court to build a new courthouse in Prineville. Outraged west siders

No other building in Central Oregon is as quickly recognized or as well known as this three-story stone structure that sits snugly in the center of the Ochoco Valley.

A band concert at a side entrance in 1910. Photo courtesy of the Crook County Historical Society.

protested. A mass rally was held in the little town of Forest to condemn the affair. When it appeared that the county court wouldn't back down, Charles Benson of Bend led a group in filing an injunction against the project, charging that it would incur new county indebtedness. Judge Bradshaw of The Dalles ruled in Benson's favor. Bradshaw ordered that no more than $5,000 of new indebtedness could be incurred. At that, the county court cancelled its first contract award and reopened the bidding, but offered the identical plans for contractors to bid on. The winning bid this time was $25,000 lower than the low bid that had previously won. This fed the already strong suspicion that court members had made an under-the-table agreement with builders in order to line their own pockets.

As a direct result of the proposed new courthouse, on January 17, 1907, a major effort was launched by west side residents to create two new counties from old Crook, to be called Jefferson and Deschutes. A long, hard-fought battle followed, with most west siders favoring division and most east siders oppos-

ing it. Jefferson County finally won the right to exist in the 1914 election, Deschutes in the 1916 election. By that time there had been a population shift to the west side and the east siders — fearing that the west could force a relocation of the county seat from Prineville to Bend if they remained inside Crook — were happy to see them go.

Meanwhile, Jack Shipp built the courthouse.

At first, Shipp had nothing to do with it. A Portland firm had won the contract, but it defaulted soon after the job began. Shipp volunteered to finish the task.

Salem architect W. D. Pugh had designed the building, but Shipp made some changes. For example, Shipp put its basement at ground level instead of in the ground the way Pugh had designed it. The reason for this change is now forgotten, but it may have been because Prineville has a high water table. The town is built atop a filled-in prehistoric lake. Much of the valley was marshland even in recent times. Some of it still is. Water can be found beneath the ground near the courthouse at a depth of only five feet. There were other changes,

too, such as having a chubbier clock tower than Pugh designed and placing a flagpole on top instead of the statue Pugh envisioned. No framing plans have been discovered for the courthouse, indicating that Pugh left it up to Shipp to figure out such details as how to attach the clock tower to the main building.

Shipp brought in the whole project for $48,591. He paid out $725 for the four-face clock that is the building's most prominent feature. The main entrance and outside doors cost a total of only six dollars. First, Shipp laid out a stone foundation, which he covered with a thin layer of dirt. He used basalt from a quarry west of Prineville for the stone on the outside of the building. For the interior paneling and fixtures, Shipp used local pine lumber, which he stained to look like oak. Indeed, people soon believed that it was oak and forgot all about the pine beneath the stain. The interior walls were also disguised. Looking like a solid 16 inches throughout, they were in fact hollow, merely pine lumber covered with plaster.

The end result was a building

The Crook County Courthouse as depicted in the painting "Historical Prineville" by Prineville folk artist Jennifer Lake Miller.

roughly 5,000 feet square, three stories high, with a three-story clock tower on top of an attic above the main building. Seven stories in all, it was the tallest building in Central Oregon. Solid-looking basalt walls overlooked a block of grass and trees, the whole enclosed with a rail fence. Cornice, frieze, and architrave work on the upper part of the building was four-and-a-half feet wide. The eight-ton tower was magnificently designed, contained barred open windows (generations of children have assumed that it is a jail with prisoners inside) and the four-faced clock. Decades have passed since a flag actually flew on the flagpole, but originally one did. There were three huge, elaborate stone entrances into the building, plus a small back door that today takes about three quarters of all the traffic. Perhaps the most stately feature of the building was the 2,268-square-foot circuit courtroom on the third floor. With its high judge's bench and witness stand, its oak-stained wainscoting and banisters, lawyers say it is one of the nicest courtrooms in Oregon.

Originally the whole government was in the building: the courts, the county departments, the school superintendent, the jail, the sheriff, and the library. As the years have passed, more and more former occupants have gone to newer buildings; however, most county offices do remain in the courthouse.

The building was remodeled in 1941 as the space crunch began to be felt. The two big stone entrances on the sides of the building were removed and replaced by interior stairs to create more office space. At other times the rail fence was removed and the big trees which had fronted the lawn were cut down. A big fountain — originally a feature of the Ochoco Inn (which burned down a quarter century ago) — was placed in front of the courthouse. A proposal to remodel again to create more courtroom space was raised in 1984, but nothing came of it. In 1985, an elevator was installed for the benefit of the handicapped and the old. It has been observed,

however, that younger citizens are more apt to use the elevator than senior citizens.

"In Danger of Collapse"

Late in 1989, courthouse building supervisor Fred Farrish noticed that things looked odd on the third floor. He called in Building Inspector Allan Coxey. Coxey, alarmed by what he saw, got County Judge Dick Hoppes' permission to call in structural engineer Norbert Volny, Jr. of Bend. What Volny saw were walls that were bowed and cracked, doors that no longer lined up, and a floor that sagged as much as two inches in places. On December 18, the courthouse was abandoned as being "in imminent danger of collapse."

A windstorm the previous October had blown the clock tower off center. Instead of resting on four columns, it now leaned slightly southeast and rested its entire eight dead tons on two posts. Volny had the tower shored up and the building was reopened on December 26. However — suspicious of the cracks he had seen — Volny took more measurements, researched the old building's original floorplan, and ran all the figures through his computer in Bend. As a result, on January 2, 1990, the courthouse was again evacuated. Volny had discovered the tower was settling into the building, and that tons of pressure were cascading through the structure all the way to the basement. Unless extensive repairs were made, the building would collapse, probably when the first strong wind gust or heavy snow hit the tower.

The crews of Volny and contractor Clint Brooks worked day and night to save the building before something happened to collapse it. A terrific windstorm blew up the Ochoco Valley January 5-7, 1990, several times creating such frightening noises in the building that workers fled in fear it was about to come down, but enough shoring had been done that the courthouse remained standing. The beautiful wainscoting was ripped out, scaffolding nailed to the stairs, and the

Continued on page 57

The "Lost" Wagon Train of Elijah Elliott

The story of the early struggle to populate the upper Willamette Valley by a wagon route through Central Oregon

In Two Parts
PART ONE

By Don Burgderfer

If you lived in the eastern United States prior to the 1860s, you had quite a trip ahead of you if you wanted to go someplace like the Eugene area of the upper Willamette Valley. Typically, you made your way overland or by steamer to Independence or St. Joseph, Missouri, and then took the Oregon Trail across the west to the promised lands west of the Cascades. That trail led you to the Columbia River east of Mt. Hood, where it was necessary to raft down the Columbia to the lower end of the Willamette Valley.

Things got a little better in 1846, for that was when Samuel Barlow began operating a shortcut toll road that passed south of Mt. Hood and went to Oregon City. But, you were still quite a distance from the *upper* Valley. So, most of the settling was taking place in the lower (northern) part of the Valley. It was a distressing situation for those folks in the upper Valley, who not only wanted to see their own lush area grow and prosper, but also wanted an easier access route to easterly markets for their produce and cattle.

Because travel was so slow and exhausting in those days, pioneers were often seeking ways to take shortcuts from the established Oregon Trail. As they arrived at the Malheur River crossing near Vale, those wanting to go to the upper Willamette Valley wondered why they should have to cut north to The Dalles via present-day Baker City and LaGrande. It seemed more logical to just simply head west. Of course, there were a couple of problems. For one thing, there was no established wagon trail westward through Central Oregon at that time. Secondly, even if they made it to the Cascades, there was no wagon route over the central Cascade Mountains.

Stephen Meek had led a wagon train in 1845 that had attempted a due-west route. But, by the time this group had reached the Wagontire Mountains (west of Harney Lake) they had lost confidence in Meek. The train splintered and wandered off in separate groups toward Sherars Bridge and The Dalles. Between 1846 and 1852, various other efforts were made to find shortcuts to the upper Willamette Valley, but all failed.

Still, the Oregon lands west of the Cascades remained attractive to would-be settlers. They had heard about the mild climate, free land, fertile valleys and relative freedom from malaria.

Work Begins On The "Free Emigrant Road"

Upper Valley residents decided to band together to mark and clear a right-of-way for a central Cascades route to be called the "Free Emigrant Road." It's possible this was the only community sponsored emigrant route in the history of western pioneer travel. They

simply *had* to have a way to attract more settlers to *their* end of the Valley. So, in March of 1852, lacking any evidence of support from the territorial government, a meeting was held in the present Springfield area.

As a result of that meeting, seven volunteers (road "viewers") responded and were to survey a route all the way to Ft. Boise (near present-day Parma). The route, if possible, was to ascend the Middle Fork of the Willamette River and then traverse the central Cascades. Actually, not much happened until July of 1852, when William Macy and John Diamond, two of the viewers, scaled the peak now called Diamond Peak and were able to look over into eastern Oregon.

On August 20, 1852, the whole group of road viewers (following a trail well known to the Indians) did go up the Middle Fork and over a new pass. The summit was a bit

south of Diamond Peak. Misfortune befell the viewers on September 15, 1852. Somewhere north of the Harney/Malheur Lakes they were attacked by Indians. Four horses were killed, three of the seven men were wounded, and their journals and geological specimens were lost. By September 23 they had made their way to the Oregon Trail at Burnt River (south of Baker) and found medical aid there. By October 20, most of the viewers had managed to return to their homes in the Valley by way of the Oregon Trail and Portland.

The viewers' report to the public indicated they had found a fine, direct route from the upper Willamette Valley to Ft. Boise, ". . . with only about 40 miles on the western descent of the Cascades needing real improvement." Curiously, no mention was made of the Indian attack. The settlers hoped that construction of the new road

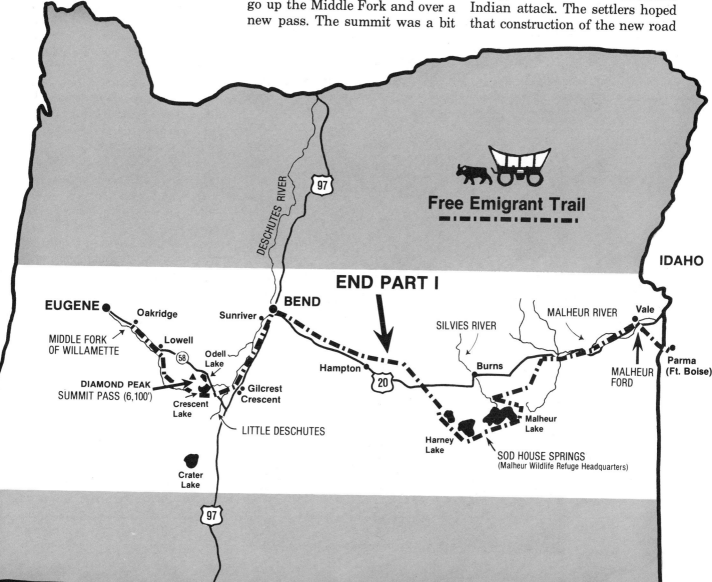

would begin early in 1853.

On March 5, 1853, a formal citizen's committee was organized at Willamette Forks to set up funding (mostly contributions) and procedures for locating, marking and building the new road, which was expected to be completed by the fall of 1853. Three road commissioners were elected: Thomas Cady, William M. Macy, and Adin G. McDowell (the latter being replaced by Asahel Spencer in June of 1853). Robert Walker was appointed road marker. And a construction contractor, Dr. Robert Alexander, was hired. It was to be a 65-day contract. The winter of 1852-53 had been a harsh one, with lots of snowpack in the mountains, but work was to start as soon as possible.

In early July of 1853, Joseph M. Garrison, a representative of the U.S. Superintendent of Indian Affairs, attempted to take a small mounted party over the new "Free Emigrant Road" and into eastern Oregon. His mission was to make treaties with hostiles along the route, in anticipation of the wagon trains that were soon to come that way. On July 9, Garrison reached a butte from which he could see the heavy snows still blanketing the high Cascade country.

At this same time he also met up with the road marker, Robert F. Walker, who was blazing the new route for the contractor, Dr. Alexander. Both Walker and Garrison agreed that their respective missions were impossible in the face of the 10 to 15-foot snowdrifts in their paths. Together, the two parties returned to the valley and went their separate ways.

In one of the ironies of this situation, it seems likely that the Walker/Garrison and the Alexander parties missed each other by only one day as they passed in opposite directions at Butte Disappointment (near present-day Lowell). So Alexander, who had begun the road construction ("clearing" is a better term) in April, was never told that Walker had given up on his road-marking project. On July 16, Alexander's party arrived at a dead-end where Walker's markings ceased. And to their great distress, no one was there.

Alexander muddled through as best he could, and even received one extension on his contract. The third contract was given to one of the road commissioners, Asahel Spencer, who reported the road finished on October 4, 1853.

On October 19, the Statesman newspaper reported the new contractor had in fact punched the new route through to the plains beyond the Deschutes and "had made a passable road of it." Inexplicably, the two other road commissioners, Cady and Macy, did not inspect Spencer's "finished" project!

Emigrants Converge

Meanwhile, the wheels of history were gaining momentum and churning relentlessly toward Oregon. From all over the east, even as far as Pennsylvania, emigrants were converging upon St. Joseph, Missouri. Some came overland, some even came by steamer up the Missouri to this jumping-off place. They came together in various sized groups. Some were tightly knit gatherings of families or neighbors. Some groups had even been so formalized as to draw up a contract regarding their responsibilities on the trek. Many more were quite loosely organized.

This wagon train, then, was not a cohesive string of wagons plodding along, one after the other. It was much more loosely constituted than that, and there were many occasions when the various wagon groups didn't even strictly follow the same trails and were often not even within sight of each other. The whole wagon train was usually strung out for a considerable distance, not in the close-knit column we are used to seeing in Hollywood movies.

In general, the trip to the Willamette Valley from Missouri was expected to take about four months. Formal information was scarce and the emigrants were warned to listen to predecessors as to best equipment, wagons and draft animals (oxen were highly favored). Everyone expected it

There is an interpretive sign on the shore of the Malheur River near the pioneer ford at Vale. From here, the emigrants followed several different trails, depending on whether they were going to California or the Willamette Valley.
Photo by Don Burgderfer

HISTORIC OREGON TRAIL
MALHEUR CROSSING
NEAR THIS SPOT WAS THE CROSSING OF THE MALHEUR BY THE OLD OREGON TRAIL. HERE PASSED THE ILL-FATED WHITMAN PARTY IN 1836, THE WEARY TRAVELERS OF THE GREAT MIGRATION IN 1843 AND IN THAT YEAR CAPTAIN FREMONT IN HIS EXPLORATIONS. THE NEARBY HOT SPRINGS OFFERED A RESTING PLACE WHERE BATHS COULD BE TAKEN AND CLOTHING WASHED.

would be an arduous journey ahead. But, few were really aware of *how* bad it was going to be.

At Ft. Boise, on the Idaho-Oregon border, the wagons from the northern and southern routes along the Snake River came together, then there was the 16-mile trek to the crossing place at the Malheur River. This was a staging area for trains going over the various Oregon Trail routes, some to The Dalles, some toward California and, uniquely *this* time, straight across Oregon on the new Free Emigrant Road.

Jane Elliott from the midwest was in one of the groups. Her husband, Elijah Elliott of Lane County, was a 35-year old Kentuckian who, like so many others, had come west without his family. In July, he left Lane County by way of Portland and here, at the Malheur crossing in late August, he made the expected rendezvous with his wife. But, he had another mission besides that to attend to.

Elijah Elliott Commissioned To Lead Group Over The New Trail

The "movers and shakers" of the upper Valley were anxious to entice as many settlers as possible over the new Free Emigrant Road and into Lane, Linn, and Benton counties. To do this, they commissioned Elijah Elliott to go to the Malheur crossing and not only tout the new route, but also lead the wagons across the state. Though there is some dispute about it, some said he was offered $500 to bring even so much as one wagon over the trail. (There are no records showing he was ever paid any sum at all.)

Elijah must have been a fairly good spokesman for the new cut-off. Of the estimated 8,000 people who were traversing the Oregon Trail at the time, about 1,000 (representing about 250 wagons) elected to follow Elliott. Many lived to regret that choice. But, in Elliott's defense, we must be quick to point out the road commissioners had assured him the new road through the central Cascades

would definitely be finished by the time his wagon train arrived there.

There was yet another problem. Elijah Elliott, though he may have been briefed somewhat by the 1852 road viewers, had never traveled the Free Emigrant Road — not any part of it! And, he was free and open in admitting this to those who followed him. So, why did anyone follow such a guide? Because the emigrants knew that if the route *were* successful, it could cut several hundred miles and weeks of travel time from the usual Oregon Trail route to the upper Valley. It sounded like an acceptable gamble to these trail-weary people.

Of course, there were scoffers who said the Free Emigrant Road was nothing but a hare-brained scheme. Some of these detractors may even have known the truth; *no* wagon, actually, had ever traveled the entire route!

Painful decisions were made at the Malheur ford. Whether to go the new cut-off route or the older (and much longer) established one. Friends and even families split on this issue. The majority were skeptical and took no chances on an untried trail and a guide who didn't seem to know much about the route on which he was embarking.

On September 1, 1853, the Elliott Cut-off train was on its way at 8:30 AM. By September 2, one child died

Painful decisions were made at the Malheur ford. Whether to go the new cut-off route or the older (and much longer) established one. The majority were skeptical and took no chances on an untried trail and a guide who didn't seem to know much about the route on which he was embarking.

The pioneer ford across the Malheur River at Vale looks far different today than it did in 1853. Now the shores are largely riprapped, several bridges cross here, and many electric irrigation pumps line the banks. It was here that Elijah Elliott met his wife and began the Elliott Cut-off adventure.
Photo by Don Burgderfer

of sickness. It must be said here that, despite all the total misery of this journey, only this child and several adult women died, one of them by drowning when a wagon overturned in a Willamette River crossing. This being said, the truth is that conditions on the trail were deplorable.

Later in the year, especially, the trail dust would rise in thick, choking clouds and infiltrate everything inside the wagons. Not only that, but the fine powder literally killed livestock and draft animals which breathed too much of it. Whenever the wagons reached good quantities of clean water, considerable effort was spent in "de-dusting" the wagons and everything in them. Even at this, though it could have been worse. During the previous year's 1852 migrations, dreaded cholera had hit the trains and an estimated 5,000 graves were left along the Oregon Trail.

The pressure to keep moving was pervasive It was September, and everyone knew it wasn't that much longer before they would have suitable weather to cross the Cascades. Knowing about the fate of the Donner party* did not quiet their fears.

Elliott party Encounters Confusion

By the time the Elliott Cut-off party had been on the road for seven or eight days, they were beginning to have their doubts about the viability of the new Free Emigrant Road. It was almost as if all the uncertainties and divisiveness of the old Meek Train were being played out again.

It didn't reassure anybody to witness Elliott's obvious uncertainty about the terrain they were in. For example, when they arrived at the Malheur/Harney Lake complex, there was much debate as to whether to pass the lakes to the north or the south. Elijah Elliott, to his credit, championed the northern Meek wagon train route of 1845, but he was voted down. The emigrants found out later that they should have listened to him. Instead, they left their encampment at the Silvies River, north of Malheur Lake, and traveled in a clockwise direction around the lake complex!

In any event, the decision to a take a southern route past the lakes turned out to be a disastrous choice leading the wagons into a soggy, torturous environment and adding at least 12 days travel time to their journey. Finally, on September 18, the train crossed the Blitzen River and headed for the west end of Harney Lake. It was during this time that some of the wagons camped at Sod House Springs, near the present Malheur Wildlife Refuge Headquarters.

Meanwhile, things were getting even worse at Elliott's wagon train. Many emigrants were getting low on food, and morale was flagging. On September

The Donner party was a group of emigrants to California who met with tragedy when they were trapped by snow in October while crossing the Sierra Nevada mountain range. The survivors were reduced to cannibalism before being rescued, and only about half the party ever reached California.

14, eight men left the train and rode ahead to go to the upper Valley and seek relief for the emigrants.

These would-be rescuers, after wasting four days getting completely turned around, finally struck out in the correct westerly direction on September 18.

Rebellion Breaks Out

Between the 18th and 20th, rebellion and threats which had been steadily simmering now broke out against Elijah Elliott. Some made actual, concrete preparations to hang him for bringing them to such a horrible place, but cooler heads prevailed and he was not hanged. Instead, he seems from this date onward to fade from historical mention as having any further leadership position in the Elliott Cut-off train. Some historians have stated he simply refused to assume any further leadership function for the the train after the rude treatment, and clear vote of "no confidence" he was given at this time.

The record suggest that Elliott, after this incident, crossed the Silvies on Meek's old trail and followed that route west for a short time. But, since no one else followed, and there was danger from Indians for a lone wagon, he turned around and rejoined the rest of the wagons on their southern route.

On September 25, 11 days after leaving the train, the advance relief party of eight riders finally reached the real Deschutes River, possibly in the vicinity of Bend. And then began another one of the insanities of this whole episode of mistakes. They thought one of the Three Sisters was Diamond Peak, which they knew should be on their route!

Incredibly, they made their difficult way to the summit between the South and Middle Sisters, only to realize that they were too far north for the Free Emigrant Road route. From the high country of the Three Sisters, they could now see to the south their objective: the real Diamond Peak.

Weakened, wet, cold, miserable, hungry, now on foot — these well-meaning souls made their way across the Chambers Lake basin and into the headwaters of the McKenzie River drainage. On October 20, they were found by local residents and their ordeal was over. But, this valiant effort turned out to be of absolutely no help to the beleaguered wagon train.

The wagons still plodded along after the eight relief riders had left. It was a mostly dry, parched desert they had to travel from Harney Lake, with great difficulties experienced in finding water at appropriate intervals. Between September 20th and 28th the train had some of its darkest hours. They were unable to find water west of Little Silver Lake and even, at one point, backtracked one 18-mile stretch to get back to a life-giving spring they had camped by earlier. For a slow-moving wagon train, it was agonizing to have to back-track like that. And with them, always, was the Donner Spectre.

The fall travel season was fading rapidly, and that barrier, the central Cascades, still lay ahead.

The "Lost" Wagon Train of Elijah Elliott

The story of the early struggle to populate the upper Willamette Valley by a wagon route through Central Oregon

In Two Parts

Along with the hardship, indecision, and rebellion in the Elliott Train as it traversed the parched high desert country over unknown roads was the growing anxiety about the rapid approach of deadly winter weather in the mountains.

By September 30, the Elliott Cutoff train had crossed Buck Creek and arrived at the South Fork of the Crooked River (on the present GI Ranch). Staying south of Bear Creek, they traversed 40 waterless miles before arriving at the Deschutes River on October 7, 1853, somewhere in or near the present-day townsite of Bend.

Paradoxically, a week before, and only 30 miles south (upstream), was Asahel Spencer's road construction crew that had made its way over the new cut-off route as far as the present-day LaPine area. They were in a position to be of inestimable help to the struggling emigrants who were approaching the final stage of their journey: ascent over the summit of the central Cascades on the totally new Free Emigrant Road.

But, with winter fast approaching, the construction party simply packed up its tools and returned to the Valley! Neither of the parties knew about the other. And so, in another unfortunate turn of fate for the emigrants, these two groups never made contact.

Wagons of the Cut-off train continued to arrive at the Deschutes encampment over the next few days. Finally, there were over 250 gathered to make the final leg of the trip. The clear, cool water of the Deschutes River was like paradise after the weary route through the central Oregon desert lands. Thirst of both animals and humans was slaked, and the de-dusting ritual was again performed, to the delight of all. Scouts were sent out to locate the section of the Free Emigrant Road that headed south from their location.

The Route from Bend

Finally, blazes were located and

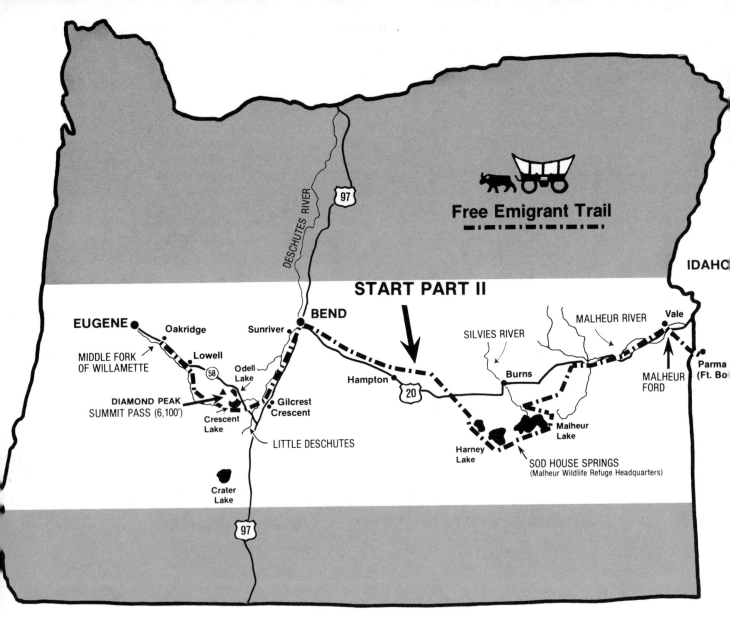

the wagons slowly started stringing south. Most historians believe the train stayed along the east bank of the Deschutes, then forded the Little Deschutes just north of the present-day settlement of Little River.

David Danley, of the Sunriver Nature Center, was almost certain the old wagon tracks went through the Sunriver area, but he could not locate them. It wasn't until he studied an aerial photograph of the 3,300 acre tract that the tracks became visible, running NE to SW for about a mile. The actual tracks were difficult to find in a ground search because the lodgepole pine grew *thicker* in the old ruts, disguising them. Sunriver has preserved a quarter-mile section of the old road as a historical site near traffic circle No. 11.

Searchers of old pioneer roads know only too well that the routes can become quite obscured, especially by logging and agricultural activities and by imposition of newer roadways. Also, the pioneers' own knowledge of local geography and place-names was frequently muddled, so their journals can often be vague or misleading. However, it is believed the Elliott train followed along Crescent Creek after fording the Little Deschutes and traveled by the north slope of Odell Butte. In fact, not too many years ago, it was said you could still see where the tracks entered the north side of Crescent Creek and emerged from the south side, 1/2 mile below the Hwy. 58 concrete bridge. (This author searched that stretch twice, but failed to find the crossing.)

Just west of Hwy. 58, Crescent Creek forks to the north and Big Marsh Creek forks south. (The pioneers called this latter creek the "West Fork of the Deschutes.") They apparently followed along the east bank of Big Marsh Creek until just east of present-day Umli, then forded the creek and headed for the Pinewan Lake vicinity, about a mile south of Crescent Lake.

Despite what one current USFS brochure tells you, the emigrants did *not* camp near present-day Spring Campground or anyplace else on the south shore of Crescent Lake. In fact, they were so hurried and pressed for time to get over the summit that it is doubtful they made many side explorations or even saw the large lake. Another USFS brochure is more accurate; it states you will cross the tracks of the Free Emigrant Road near Pinewan Lake, which is about a mile south of Crescent Lake.

Beyond the west end of Crescent Lake, the wagons moved northward, crossing the present Forest Road #6010 (the Summit Lake road) several miles west of Crescent Lake and NE of Meek Lake. They then headed generally westward, going over the Cascade summit near the southern slope of Diamond Rockpile.

Just west of Diamond Rockpile they went around the headwaters of Emigrant Creek and headed down Pioneer Gulch, connecting with the present Forest Road #6010 near where Indigo Creek enters the Middle Fork of the Willamette River. Thus, it may be seen that this pioneer train did not in any way follow Road #6010 between Crescent and Summit Lakes, nor did it cross the summit at Emigrant Pass, as one might have suspected from the name.

In fact, road #6010 follows a road established in the middle 1860s, and it was called the Oregon Central Military Road. The OCMR did, in many places, take over the Elli-

ott Cut-off track and obliterate it, as have some of the other, more recent forest roads. Certain portions of Forest Roads #6010, 60 and 6020 near Summit and Crescent Lakes often follow the old 1867 OCMR route.

One can imagine the joy with which the emigrants finally realized they were at the Middle Fork of the Willamette River! From here they needed only to follow the Middle Fork to Butte Disappointment (near present-day Lowell) and thence to the upper Valley. And no more would there be any shortages of water.

Little did they realize what lay ahead!

Cry for Help

Because people of the train were tired, hungry, and short of supplies (especially flour), a rider had been sent on ahead to Butte Disappointment to seek help. He was a young schoolmaster, Martin Blanding. He reached Butte Disappointment on October 16, several days before the train began the rigors of travel over the new Cascade summit pass. Blanding, weakened and practically starved, was found by two young people who had seen his campfire smoke as he was preparing to eat a young colt at his

encampment. (He was completely unaware of the settlement's proximity at the time.)

Blanding related the plight of the long-awaited Elliott wagon train to the local residents. His own appearance and condition were sufficient reason for serious concern about his fellow emigrants. He was, truly, the hero of the hour.

What happened next is one of the most heart-warming sagas in the annals of western pioneer history. Riders went out all over the upper Valley to spread the word that the Elliott party was on the track but was in serious trouble and needed help. The area residents mounted a massive rescue effort, collecting thousands of pounds of flour, fatted beef cattle for slaughtering, and other rations for the struggling emigrants.

This was a joint effort of the estimated 2,000 or so citizens of Lane, Linn, and Benton Counties. After all, this was *their* wagon train, the one they had worked so hard to promote and bring to reality, the one that was going to open the backdoor of the Willamette Valley to the westward emigration movement.

In a matter of eight days, in late October, 1853, 94 pack animals and 23 loaded wagons and various beef cattle were on their way to the Elli-

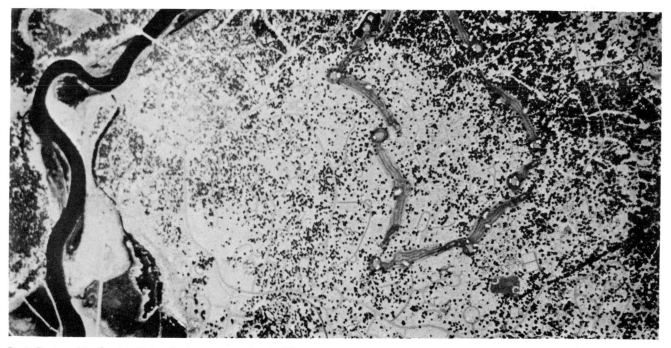

David Danley, of the Sunriver Nature Center, was sure that the Elliott party had travelled through the Sunriver location in 1853, but couldn't find the track. However, when he examined an aerial photograph of Sunriver, the track became visible. It is the dark line of trees at the right center of photo. The Deschutes River is to the west (left side of photo). Photo by Don Burgderfer.

The old wagon track at Sunriver was not betrayed by visible ruts in the ground (as is common in Eastern Oregon). Instead, the almost 140-year-old trail was revealed in an aerial photo by the lodgepole pines which germinated more densely in the compacted soil of the wagon tracks. The trees at left are well lined up in the track. This area has been preserved by Sunriver as a historical site. Photo by Don Burgderfer

ott train. First contact with the forerunners of the train had been made on October 19. By October 23, the stretched-out bulk of the Elliott train had found the new route over the Cascades and was on the trail toward their approaching rescuers.

Actually, the emigrants had been eating quite a bit of meat (their own livestock and draft animals, unfortunately), but what they most craved was bread! It is reported the rescuers ended up cooking vast quantities of pancakes for the bread- and flour-starved emigrants!

The rescue mission was also a real eye-opener for the residents of the upper Valley. They had previously believed the newspaper accounts of the finished status of the new Free Emigrant Road. Now they were able to see first-hand for themselves what a deplorable condition the "road" was in.

The road from Bend to LaPine had been little more than blazes, and once the route entered timbered areas, the trees were hardly cut in a sufficiently wide swath to admit wagon travel. On the west side, along the Middle Fork, it was even worse. Huge fir trees were down across the road. Instead of cutting a path through them, the road contractors had made flimsy log bridges over them! This was a

precarious situation for the wagons, which often had to be pushed over the ramps by hand. Sometimes the wagons toppled over in the process. This was not what the emigrants or citizens had been led to expect!

Rescued at Big Pine Opening

About seven miles west of Indigo Creek, on the Middle Fork, is Big Pine Opening, a meadow. The rescuers had reached early elements of the train by the time this area had been reached by the wagons. More painful decisions for the emigrants were at hand. The winter snows of early November were imminent. Time was of the essence. The Donner party* was on everyone's mind. The rescuers prevailed upon many of the emigrants to simply abandon their wagons at this place, cache their possessions, and proceed on foot or animal as quickly as possible to the safety of the Valley.

Not all of the emigrants were willing to abandon everything they

*The Donner party was a group of emigrants to California who met with tragedy when they were trapped by snow in October while crossing the Sierra Nevada mountain range. The survivors were reduced to cannibalism before being rescued, and only about half the party ever reached California.

had lugged across the western plains. Some did leave their wagons and household possessions along this part of the trail; some did not. Many did not realize the seriousness of what the rescuers now knew: the route along the Middle Fork was not a "road." Worse, it would necessarily cross that river *27 times* before they arrived at Butte Disappointment! One pioneer lady died on this stretch when her wagon capsized at one of the hazardous crossings.

As a result of the above, many of the settlers arrived in the Valley practically destitute, with no wagon, no possessions, no livestock, no funds — virtually nothing except the clothes on their backs. Others arrived in relatively good shape. Some few had wisely shipped household goods by steamer to the west coast. Many who had cached belongings at Big Pine Opening or other places subsequently found those goods stolen.

At least the emigrants knew one thing: they had moved in with some mighty fine neighbors!

The first of the wagons reached Fall Creek in the upper Willamette Valley on October 24, 1853. This was about 55 days after they had left the Vale area. Rescue efforts to bring in the remainder of the Elliott train were not completed until mid-November. The train had traveled over 500 miles from Ft. Boise. On the plus side of the ledger, they had experienced only one minor Indian incident (unlike the tragic Clark party two years earlier) and had suffered only three or so deaths during the journey. In light of the 1851 and 1852 wagon train experiences with Indians and cholera, that was an exceptionally good record!

It has been variously estimated that the arrival of the Elliott train increased the population of the upper Willamette Valley by one-third to one-half! One count of the emigrants who actually came out of the Middle Fork valley was: 615 men, 412 women and children, 3,970 cattle, 1,700 sheep, 222 horses, and 64 mules. There is apparently no concise record of how many in each category *started* the journey at Vale.

However, the experiences of the Elliott train and their magnificent rescuers did make it clear to the valley residents that the Free Emigrant Road had been sorely misrepresented. It was poorly located and even more poorly cleared. In 1854, some of the deficiencies were corrected, and it was noted that an 1854 wagon train led by William Macy (one of the original road viewers, and one who had been wounded by Indians) led about 100 wagons from Vale in only about 40 days, taking the northern route above Harney/Malheur basin instead of the treacherous southern route taken by the Elliott dissidents.

Despite Macy's successful trip in 1854, the handwriting was on the wall for the Free Emigrant Route. By 1855, the Kansas and Oklahoma territories were opening up, and they were a lot easier for emigrants to get to than remote Oregon. By 1862 the McKenzie route over the Cascades was opened up, and the Elliott route then became little more than a pack trail and a way to get Valley livestock to the lush Crescent Creek/upper Deschutes grazing meadows.

In the middle 1860s the Oregon Central Military Road was surveyed and constructed (finished in 1867). That road frequently followed and obliterated the Free Emigrant Road, especially along the Middle Fork. In modern times, portions of the Middle Fork route are lost to the impounded waters of reservoirs such as Hills Creek, Lookout Point, and Dexter.

The summit pass utilized by the Elliott train, just south of Diamond Rockpile, was over 6,100 feet in elevation. Locators of the 1867 OCMR found a pass just north of Summit Lake (now USFS Road #6010) that was only 5,600 feet in elevation. On July 27, 1865, Bynon Pengra and W.H. Odell visited Odell Lake. Mr. Pengra, Surveyor General of Oregon, confirmed his belief that at the west end of this lake was a pass even lower than Emigrant Pass on the OCMR. He was right. The present-day Willamette Pass on Hwy. 58 is only a bit over 5,100 feet in elevation, about 500 feet lower than Emigrant Pass, and about 1,000 feet lower in elevation than that sad trail taken by the Elliott wagon train of 1853. Just southwest of Willamette Pass, at the west end of Odell Lake, is Pengra Pass, even lower yet at only 5,003 feet elevation, and it is this pass which is now used by the Southern Pacific Railroad.

Elijah Elliott assumed a place in Oregon pioneer history that few would envy. Yet, it seems unjust to refer to this affair as the *"Elliott Lost Wagon Train."* From the time the train left the Harney basin, Elliott had become a follower, not a leader. And those who led the train from then on knew no more about the route than did Elijah.

It is entirely possible that Mr. Elliott should be ranked as one of the most naive fall-guys we have ever run into in our history books. He was probably wrong to assume he could lead a wagon train over a route of which he had no personal knowledge. But, others must also share in the blame for this extraordinary exploitation of eager emigrants.

What of Robert Walker, who was supposed to mark out the route for Dr. Alexander's construction crew? He left his job and never even told anyone. Dr. Alexander didn't finish his job, even with a contract extension. And, apparently he didn't do a very decent job of what he did finish. Then, road commissioner Asahel Spencer took over the contract and eventually gave out ballyhoo to newspapers such as the *Statesman* that the road was "finished and passable." That was a patent lie, as the emigrants sadly found out.

And what of the other two road commissioners, Thomas Cady and William Macy? Neither one ever bothered to inspect the so-called "finished" product, though Macy would have been eminently quali-fied to do so since he was one of the original road viewers.

Out of eagerness, indolence, deception, or ignorance, Cady and Macy willingly accepted, without verification, Spencer's announcements of a finished, passable road. And, to make it worse, they did not even designate one of the original road viewers to lead the first wagon train over the untried track. Instead, in Elijah Elliott they found a willing, gullible shill.

I think it is fair to assume that Elijah Elliott thought he was dealing with responsible, upright men of honor. They said the route would be finished when he arrived there, and he believed them. Perhaps he was also offered money, perhaps not. But, knowing his wife was on the incoming train, he was hardly in a mood to quibble about that.

If Elijah is to be faulted at all, perhaps he *was* too eager to lead where he had never led before. But, to his eternal good credit, he was completely honest about that with every man he met. ■

FOR MAPS AND INFORMATION:
Willamette National Forest
Rigdon Ranger Station
49098 Salmon Creek Road
Oakridge, OR 97463
(503) 782-2283
Deschutes National Forest
Crescent Ranger District
P.O. Box 208
Crescent, OR 97733
(503) 433-2234

ACKNOWLEDGEMENTS:
Most of this article is a painfully brief condensation of a research project titled "Cutoff Fever," appearing in six issues of the *Oregon Historical Quarterly*, December 1976 through Spring 1978. That material was written by a grand historian who died in 1988, Leah Collins Menefee, with co-author Lowell Tiller. Preliminary editing of that material was done by Keith and Donna Clark.

I am also indebted to Edward Gray, author of *An Illustrated History of Early Klamath County, Oregon*. He spent many happy hours discussing history at Leah Menefee's knee, so to speak, and gives valued details in the above book as to locations and other aspects of the Free Emigrant Road.

Finally, I am, as usual, grateful to the gracious workers at the Deschutes County Historical Society, who have so willingly provided their time and materials to this author.

The Legend of BILL BROWN

Though famous as "the millionaire horse king," Bill Brown became a legend in his own time for his odd behavior, philosophical observations, and his charities.

By David Braly

A thin, white-bearded man dressed in country garb walked into a Burns drugstore one day almost a century ago. He asked the clerk for strychnine. The clerk put a bottle of the deadly poison on the counter. The man took a pocket knife, pried off the cork, dipped his blade into the poison, then lifted it to his lips and (to the clerk's horror) tasted it.

"I ought to have the law on you for selling such stuff," said the man. "It wouldn't kill a tick."

The joke was that it should have killed just about anything. But, as Bill Brown explained to his friends when he recounted the incident, he believed he had developed an immunity to small amounts of strychnine by consuming tiny particles that got on his raisins. Brown used strychnine on carcasses to kill the coyotes that fed on them. He carried the poison bottle in the same pocket as the raisins he habitually munched on.

Stories about Bill Brown doing strange things were common during his lifetime and became abundant after his death. Any way you figured it, Brown was a strange one. Starting from scratch in the sheep business, he became the West's "millionaire horse king." His livestock roamed across five counties. Yet it was not as a tycoon alone that he became a legend in his own lifetime. His odd behavior, his philosophical observations and his charities also contributed to Brown's fame. Ironically, a man viewed as wise by his contemporaries became the object of derision after his death, when people repeated such tales as the one about how Brown had bought his own saddle horse from a thief three times without recognizing it. Brown never did that. He knew his own saddle horse. But he could only guess how many horses he possessed.

Brown owned ranches in Crook, Harney, and Lake counties, grazed sheep in Grant County and had horses running free in Deschutes County. He owned 36,000 acres of land. By possession of waterholes, he controlled another 100,000 acres. A store, stock camps, corrals, and warehouses were built on the land, and at his peak Brown owned 8,000 to 10,000 horses and 22,000 sheep.

He did peak, though. Brown died broke. And that is ironic because he sweated bullets to build an empire from a small homestead on Wagontire Mountain.

* * *

Bill Brown was 27 when he arrived at Wagontire Mountain in 1882. The former school teacher had set out from Oregon City with his brothers George and Bob seeking good rangeland. Each man had about $2,700 to invest. They rode up above Pendleton into eastern Washington, then through Central Oregon into California. Of all the country they saw, they preferred Wagontire Mountain.

They filed homestead claims there and bought sheep. That first winter they camped between a mountain outcropping and their fire. It was miserable. The next winter they at least had tents and a camp stove. Eventually they gathered enough logs to build a cabin.

Then came the bitter winter of 1884-85. The brothers had more than 4,000 sheep when the winter began and only 700 when it ended. George and Bob wanted out. Bill wanted to stay. So Bill bought out his brothers for their original investments. He had no money, but they accepted his promise to pay them and departed.

None of the brothers regretted the bargain. Bob became a big potato farmer at Klamath Falls and George an Oregon City banker. There were two other brothers: Sam, a farmer, and Ellis, a Portland doctor. But Bill became the most successful.

The success came hard. He had to fight the elements, predators, and cattlemen. Decades later, guests in his house would be rudely roused from their sleep by the nightmares of their host as he cried: "Coyote! Coyote!" During the Crook County range war, masked gunmen slaughtered 500 of his sheep near Hampton Buttes. Usually Brown took his losses philosophically. When a newly-hired 15-year-old herder had to watch 5,000 sheep alone, Brown uttered no reproach upon discovering that in a few days coyotes and the elements had killed 1,600 of the sheep.

Brown soon had claims staked to parcels in several counties. Although headquartered at his big house on Buck Creek, other areas became associated with him: Fife, Gap, Lost Creek, Freezeout, and of course Wagontire. He bought many waterhole sections on the cheap from a wagon road company. In later years, Brown also bought claims of would-be homesteaders who gave up.

Barely had Brown established himself as a sheep rancher when he diversified. The horse market had gone soft. Horse raisers were selling out. Brown believed the market would rebound. He began buying horses. Their owners thought they were outsmarting Brown when they sold him desert nags for $2.50 to $10 a head. He bought entire herds.

Brown later purchased top quality Morgan studs for his desert mares. They produced horses preferred by the U.S. Cavalry.

Every fall Brown and his wranglers drove hundreds of unbroken horses over the McKenzie Pass to Eugene and other Willamette Valley towns. Buyers showed up at corrals. When a buyer spotted a horse he liked, he made an offer. Then Brown would begin to "dicker," a favorite pastime of his. When buyers in one town had bought all the wild horses they could handle, Brown and his wranglers headed for the next town north.

In later years, Brown held private auctions at his own ranch. At one, he sold 500 geldings for $100 each and 385 mares for $85 each. These horses descended from those he'd bought for as little as $2.50.

*O*ne woman asked Brown why he always sought a young woman instead of a woman his own age. "If you want a good dog you get it when it's a pup and train it," he explained.

Brands concerned Brown. He bought every horse carrying certain brands, and vented the brands on horses he sold. He preferred his own Horseshoe Bar brand. He never sold a Horseshoe Bar horse in Central Oregon. If such a horse were found in Central Oregon, only Brown could claim it. He even had tiny Horseshoe Bar irons made for branding his sheep on their noses.

He altered the brand slightly each year in seven-year cycles so he would know the age of any of his sheep just by looking at its nose.

Even though he became famous as "the millionaire horse king," Brown himself paid little attention to the horses. They roamed freely the High Desert and the mountains. His foreman and wranglers watched them while Brown watched his sheep. Perhaps, as one writer suggested, he preferred the quiet and solitude of a herder's life to the hussle of a wrangler's.

***

Endurance was a Brown trait. It has been claimed that even in his late seventies Brown would work all day and after supper walk the 20 miles from his Gap ranch to his house at Buck Creek.

A thin, broad-shouldered man who stood six feet, Brown was as mild-mannered as he was strong-bodied. Brown did not swear, smoke, chew tobacco drink, gamble, or use slang. He took pride in being celibate. Totally honest himself, he accepted others as the same until they gave him cause to think otherwise. Brown was charitable but personally austere, fair but not always a good judge of people.

"I don't know of any man that I ever knew that was more fair than Brown or as honest as he was," recalled a former foreman, Fred Houston.

One of Brown's many oddities was that he never wore boots at a time and in a place where rural men always did. He wore brograns. In an interview on file at Prineville's Bowman Museum, Houston recalled that Brown would unlace his shoes before mounting a horse so that his feet would not get caught in the stirrup if the animal threw him. A writer 50 years ago asserted that Brown sometimes rode horses in his stocking feet. Everyone agreed that the "horse king" had so little knowledge of a horse's endurance that he rode long distances at great speed, nearly killing the animal.

***

Brown built a big house on Buck Creek. Included among its 14 or 15 rooms was a nursery for future Browns after he found a strong young woman to marry. But Brown wanted even his house to turn a profit. He laid in $10,000 worth of merchandise in a big room for sale to wranglers, neighbors, and travelers.

At first the store made money. He had a manager run it for several years, and later one of his sisters did it. After she left, Brown operated it in his own peculiar fashion. When he couldn't find an item's price, Brown dickered. And that could be costly. He once sold a tent for $7.50 and later found that invoice that showed he'd bought it for $15 in Portland. Another time he lost the price tag for calico. Normally sold by the yard, Brown figured up the cost of its wool, weaving, transportation, and other values, then sold it by the pound. Housewives quickly bought it out at his bargain price.

Brown extended credit to everyone in the area. Their word, recalled Houston, was "as good as gold."

Other stories about Brown and his store are less reliable. Some may be true. Brown allegedly used a box instead of a cash register, allowed customers to keep their own accounts and make their own change, occasionally weighed produce by lifting it in his hands instead of using the scales, and jotted down sales on scraps of paper, shoebox lids, or anything else handy. One story is that Brown ordered a wagon load of women's shoes — all the same size.

Once Brown came upon two teenagers making off with a load of groceries stolen from his store. The boys fled into the sagebrush. Brown tore the wiring out of their car engine, then went for the sheriff. While he was gone, the marooned boys smashed the cans and cut open the flour sacks in a frantic effort to destroy the evidence. It did them no good. A Prineville judge fined them. Although no reimbursement had been ordered for Brown, he gave the boys jobs so they could pay their fines.

Tales of Brown's incompetent storekeeping abound. There are numerous — if dubious — stories about wranglers and homesteaders stealing from him right under his nose. Even many factual stories have been embellished.

Governor Oswald West once stayed at the Buck Creek house while on his way to a conference in Idaho. He recalled:

"The ranch house was large and roomy, but Bill's bedroom, of which I was to become a joint occupant, was quite small and hardly afforded room for its double bed and a desk which occupied one corner. The desk was littered with, and surrounded by, check stubs, which appeared to be Bill's only method of bookkeeping.

"When it came time to retire, I found that Bill, my sleepmate, had been wearing red woolen underwear (it was hot July) while hay making and had perspired quite freely."

Brown charged the governor 50¢ for stabling his horse and the same amount for use of half his bed.

Eventually Brown stopped carrying merchandise in his store. Instead, area residents place orders, he ordered from a wholesaler, and he had a truck deliver the shipment to the customer's house. He charged expenses only and often took payment in beef.

West's mention of Brown's check stubs should have ended the myth that Brown only used tomato can labels and scraps of paper for checks. Brown carried and used a checkbook. He never carried cash, fearing he might be mugged.

But when Brown ran out of checks, he did jot payments on anything handy. Paper torn from a ruled tablet, a corner of a newspaper, a piece of wallpaper, and yes, the backs of tomato can labels, became checks which banks honored. He wrote at least one check on a wooden shingle and another on a an 8" x 12" inside part of a sheep hide.

***

Brown always intended to marry, preferably a young, strong woman to produce healthy sons to fill his empty nursery. But he was too busy building his business when he was young, and no young woman wanted him when he was old.

Brown allegedly tried to court a young woman in Harney County. He had a gold necklace made for her which bore his famous Horseshoe Bar brand. Brown put it around her neck and told her, "I've got my brand on you." She threw it on the floor. After this incident, his wranglers composed a poem poking fun at Brown.

One woman asked Brown why he always sought a young woman instead of a woman his own age. "If you want a good dog you get it when it's a pup and train it," he explained.

Brown did dress up for dances and do some courting. But he never married, apparently never even slept with a woman. He regretted his lack of sons. With sons, he believed he could "own the whole state of Oregon."

Brown shared. He is said to have given Christmas gifts to every woman and child in his vicinity. Homesteaders who broke backs and spirits trying to farm the high desert found a friend in Bill Brown. He loaned them horses, gave them jobs, and made sure their families had enough to eat.

Brown loaned $3,000 to build the Methodist church in Prineville. On the day of its dedication, Brown appeared and tore up the note.

He endowed a Methodist home in New Jersey and a Catholic church in Lakeview. He gave $10,000 to an academy in Pendleton, another $10,.000 to the Willamette University School of Music, at least that much to the Methodist Old Folks Home in Salem, and endowments to several girls' schools.

World War I made big money for Bill Brown. Allied cavalries needed horses. He had exactly the sort they wanted. He held auctions twice in two years and averaged $87 a horse from American and Canadian government agents ... about $100,000.

The Depression caught him over-extended. Also, the army had gone to armor transport and farmers to tractors; the only remaining market for Brown's horses was as cured meat for foreigners and feed for chickens. He hated selling horses as food, but believed that he had no choice.

In 1930, Houston gathered 1,013 horses for him and drove them to Bend. Placed in freight cars and shipped to Portland, they became chicken feed. Other roundups followed until all were gone.

Brown decided to retire to the Methodist Old Folks Home in Salem. Although he had helped to endow it, he had not reserved a place for himself and had no money to buy one. His brothers paid the $1,000 necessary to get him in. He remained there until his death January 11, 1941.

The legend has survived the man. Even today Bill Brown stories are told on the high desert and Wagontire Mountain. ■

walls stripped of their plaster to reveal the building's 80-year-old wooden frame. While workers pounded and sawed from the basement to the tower, a thick layer of sawdust and concrete dust settled on everything inside the huge building, including the Christmas trees which had been put up before the first evacuation.

By the time county employees moved back into the building in mid-April 1990, Brooks had put everything back to normal. Indeed, the plaster and some other features looked even better than before. Brook's' son Jody invented a hand roller to apply artificial oak grain to the stained pine. Clear Pine Mouldings managed to copy 1909-style molded lumber, taking 16 hours to cut six sets of knives for it, and then their workers went in on their days off to install it. Although they knew it would not be in a public area, the Clear Pine crew saw to it that the boards contained no knots or fingerjoints.

In danger of collapse, the Crook County courthouse was evacuated, and crews worked day and night to save the building.

The total cost of the repairs was $141,312.22. The original estimate of repair cost had been $300,000 to $600,00. The county saved lots of money taking volunteer contributions like Clear Pine's. Some of the labor was provided by jail prisoners who volunteered. Brooks, too, kept his costs down and looked for ways to save the county money. Not all of the courthouse was repaired — the third floor still sags in places — but it was made safe and presentable.

Today Central Oregon's best known building is again open for business — and for visits. The clock tower is off limits to tourists, although some exceptions are made for organized groups. Generations of school children have ascended the tall tower to see the clockworks, look out over the Ochoco Valley, and add their names to the graffiti that covers the interior. But it is possible again for people to examine the basalt walls, the fine wainscoting, the great lobby, and appreciate anew the building skills of that earlier generation, and what $48,591 used to buy. ■

Over The River And Up The Hill

*A Marine combat engineer's personal account
of his 17-week training camp
at Fort Abbot near Sunriver in 1943*

By Howard R. Simpson

"**M**en," the bow-legged captain from Georgia told us, "you've been chosen to become combat engineers . . . infantrymen with brains." It sounded vaguely ominous but we were too tired to worry. It was 0300 on a misty Oregon morning in the fall of 1943. We'd arrived at Camp Abbot, near Bend, after a long bus ride from the Klamath Falls train depot. Most of us were draftees. Three weeks at the Presidio of Monterey had almost convinced us we were soldiers. We flopped on the double decker bunks, hoping to catch some sleep before reveille.

During the trip from California I'd tried to understand what logic had brought me to this Camp high in the Cascade mountains. I'd requested assignment to the Amphibious Engineers. I'd watched them training on the beach at Santa Cruz that summer. This, I'd thought, was the outfit for me. Sun, sea, sand, and groups of shapely bathers watching us as the landing craft circled offshore and turned into the surf for practice

runs. When a staff sergeant had announced my posting to the Engineers I'd assumed I'd soon be joining the Amphibs. Now, the fact that the nearest body of water to Camp Abbot was the Prineville reservoir convinced me a grave typing error had been made on my orders.

Our sleep ended abruptly when a sergeant rattled his walking stick along the row of bunks. Formed up for the first time as a company, we blinked in the sunlight, surveying our new environment. It was definitely mountain country. Scrub pines surrounded the barracks, volcanic dust had already dulled the shine on our boots. The officers and non-coms charged with turning us into Combat Engineers over the next 17 weeks eyed us with a marked lack of enthusiasm. We were a mixed bag: high school graduates; construction workers; college graduates who hadn't joined the ROTC or had waited too long to apply for OCS; Indians from Montana and Wyoming; blue-collar workers from San Francisco and Seattle; Hispanics from Southern California; and a few drifters who hadn't moved far enough or fast enough to outrun the envelope

bearing "greetings" from the President of the United States.

We spent the first few days at close order drill and dusty three mile hikes. We were issued our equipment, including a training rope to be slung over our shoulders and worn on all occasions as the badge of a Combat Engineer. Our captain told us we'd been honored by selection into the great tradition of military engineering. He did his best to instill an esprit de corps, lecturing us on the importance of our mission and the history of our Arm. He spoke of the origins of the Corps, its links with the French military engineers dating from the Revolutionary War, the bond between the U.S. Marines and the Corps since their combat partnership in World War I, and spoke of the pride we should feel at wearing the crenelated castle on our lapels.

We were issued M1 rifles during our second week and training began in earnest as winter approached and a cool wind whistled down from the peaks. It soon became obvious the engineers spent a lot of their time insuring that the rest of the Army got where it wanted to go and denying the enemy the same privilege. It was

*F*ormed up for the first time as a company, we blinked in the sunlight, surveying our new environment. It was definitely mountain country. Scrub pines surrounded the barracks, volcanic dust had already dulled the shine on our boots.

During World War II this symbolic log structure stood at the entrance to U.S. Army Engineers' Camp Abbot, a training center which covered a sizeable part of what is now Sunriver.

hard work. We built bridges, then we blew them. We dug tank traps, then we filled them. We laid mines, then we dug them up. We learned to walk away from fizzing set charges when we would have preferred to sprint for the nearest cover. We were introduced to the fast-flowing Deschutes River. It was hate at first sight. The enemy may have been waiting for us in Europe and the Pacific but the roiling Deschutes became our real antagonist. Its broad, dark surface taunted us as we launched assault boats. It dispersed our pontoons when we tried to put a bridge together, it snapped the lines of our narrow infantry footbridges and carried them downstream like splintered boxwood.

Then the snow came. The first blizzard dropped a foot of white silence on the camp. The potbellied stoves in the barracks burned day and night, laying a fine coke dust over the drifts. Any hope the winter conditions would bring a slackening in our training schedule were dashed when we were ordered to fall out for a five mile hike during a heavy snowstorm. The captain explained that winter training was a great opportunity. Learning to live and fight in the snow, he told us, would be better than sweating it out in a Nevada desert or being eaten alive by mosquitos in Texas or Florida. He hinted that our winter expertise would guarantee us a European assignment rather than banishment to some snake-ridden island in the South Pacific.

We learned to survive in the snow. We used TNT to break the frozen ground, dug our foxholes, covered them with shelter halves and waited for a fresh snowfall to provide an insulated roof. We broke thick ice with concussion grenades — taking some trout as a bonus — to anchor the foundations of our bridges and discovered how quickly weapons and explosives malfunctioned in freezing temperatures. One cold early morning during a field exercise I came off sentry duty and crawled into my warm, snow-covered hole to sleep. Hours later I emerged to find myself completely alone. A new storm had obliterated all traces of my occupancy and the battalion, its strength down by one, had moved off while I slept.

Gradually, our squad took on a certain cohesion. We worked together as a team. Our experiences and shared hardships pulled us together. Individual shortcomings were recognized and attempts made to surmount them. A chubby trainee who always lagged behind on the obstacle course was assigned two helpers who saw him through the ordeal and brought him to the finish on time. My chronic inability to tie a dependable knot was quickly recognized. This skill is important to a Combat Engineer, particularly during river crossings. By common agreement and a mutual desire for self-preservation the squad relieved me of all knot tying duties. In exchange, I assisted others to draw maps during our reconnaissance missions.

We learned to live together as a social unit by setting our own rules. A member of the squad who spurned hot water and soap until his presence constituted a health hazard became a reluctant presence in the showers after experiencing a classic "dry scrub" with a stiff brush. We knew the "Chief," a powerful, taciturn Cheyenne from Montana and his tribal companions from other squads, were not to be disturbed or approached on Saturday nights when they hid under the barracks to drink their weekly case of Lucky Tiger hair tonic.

Gradually we grew more proficient at soldiering and physically tougher. The route marches with full field equipment increased to 10 and 15 miles. The combat courses under live fire accustomed us to the lethal snap of bullets and the earth's protective qualities. We listened skeptically to an instructor explain how easy it was to disable an armored vehicle with bazooka rounds and molotov cocktails. We made our own grenades with TNT blocks, nails, and adhesive tape. The Regulars in charge of the camp's heavy weapons section sent us floundering through the snowdrifts under the weight of heavy machine guns and tapping our bursts of curving tracers at distant targets. A bayonet instructor with a cherubic face made us jog through the course twice because our shouts and growls weren't fierce enough. During a thrust and parry drill with unsheathed bayonets I suffered the only wound

The film had been designed to impress wavering neutral nations and to frighten Germany's enemies. It certainly had achieved its basic goal that dark, depressing day in Oregon.

I was destined to receive in World War II. It was a miniscule cut on one finger that speckled the snow with blood and sent me off to the medics for "treatment."

One exercise took us into a national game preserve where the deer were plentiful, curious and surprisingly unafraid. We had been on a diet of C and K rations and were suddenly haunted by visions of roast venison. The temptation proved too much for our sergeant. Face to face with an inquisitive buck, he drew his .45 and opened fire at point blank range, missing the target completely. It was a humiliating debacle but one of the company's best marksman was later sent out as a hunter and we soon had venison joints sizzling over our fires.

Disheartened By German Training Film

Three days before Christmas we were marched to a large auditorium. We expected another boring training film but this promised to be different. The presenting officer wore the Purple Heart and a campaign ribbon studded with battle stars. *He* had been there. We hung on his every word. He explained we were about to see a captured German training film showing *their* sappers in action. He suggested we watch carefully.

The lights went down, Teutonic script flickered on the screen and our German counterparts came into focus. They all seemed to be tall, blond, and very tough. Their assault crossings were models of efficiency. They destroyed enemy pillboxes with a minimum of effort under perfect covering fire. Their bridges seemed to leap across rivers with miraculous ease. Their satchel charges opened enemy tanks as if they were made of cheap tin. Their physical prowess was unbelievable. They jumped and tumbled down rocky ravines, swam streams loaded down with heavy equipment and went into their final attack light-footed and exaltant as a German marching song swelled in volume.

When the lights came up there was complete silence. The Army, in its eagerness to display "The Face Of The Enemy" had succeeded in scaring the hell out of us. In comparison to the sappers in *feldgrau* we looked like a troop of Boy Scouts. Our morale deflated like a punctured balloon. We marched back to the barracks wondering if a few more months of training might be a good idea. The effects of the screening wore off gradually. It was only after the war that the truth was revealed. It *was* a captured film about German assault engineers. But it also happened to be a propaganda effort produced by the *Wermacht*, using selected actors, circus performers and stuntmen. Many takes had ensured a flawless performance. The film had been designed to impress wavering neutral nations and frighten Germany's enemies. It had certainly achieved its basic goal that dark, depressing day in Oregon.

Our "Graduation" Exercise

Our training was to end with a two day, battalion-size operation including a river crossing in assault boats, an attack on enemy held heights, and a 25 mile march back to camp. It was to be our graduation" exercise. We were told a general and his staff from Fort Belvoir would witness our effort. We'd be using live ammunition on prepositioned targets and moving forward under supporting fire from the heavy weapons sections. The battalion had already lost one man on the firing range and another had drowned during a river crossing. We were warned to be particularly careful.

At 0530 on the fateful morning we were in position on the right bank of the Deschutes, hidden from sight in the heavy brush. Spring had made its timid appearance and the snow was beginning to melt. The river rushed past, tossing uprooted trees like matchsticks. The assault boats were ready, bow-on to the muddy water. We were ready, helmeted and laden with bandoleers of ammunition, slung M1s, bayonets, grenades, clumsy gas masks, and our ubiqui-

Illustration by Howard R. Simpson

tous training ropes. Our jumping-off signal was to be a burst of fire from the .30 caliber water-cooled machine gun positioned on the nearby bridge. Earlier, moving to the river, we'd caught a glimpse of the general and his entourage. They too were on the bridge, scanning the opposite bank with binoculars. Tense and eager, we waited.

For some unexplained reason a whistle blast broke the silence. It wasn't the burst of fire we were waiting for but two assault boat crews — in a reflex action — began to push off. Officers shouted and non-coms roared to abort the premature action. The flustered crews manhandled their craft back under cover. We could only guess what this tactical *faux pas* must have looked like from the bridge.

Finally, the firing began. We slid the boats over the mud into the water, clambered in and manned our stubby paddles, trying to set a smooth rhythm. The Deschutes was decidedly uncooperative. We slid downstream in the heavy current. We redoubled our efforts, producing an uncontrollable spin that pointed the bow back to shore. All around us other assault boats were twirling like disoriented water bugs. The covering fire continued, throwing up fountains of dirty snow on the far bank. Now we were paddling madly upstream but inexorably moving in the opposite direction.

Our objective faded from sight. The officers on the bridge became distant onlookers. Luckily, a curve in the river had formed a long finger of silt. We ran aground and debarked in water up to our knees. It took 20 minutes to work our way back through the scrub and fallen trees to where we were supposed to have landed. The officer tried to salvage the battalion's honor, sorting the tangle of men into companies, platoons, and squads. In the real world of combat we would have all been Purple Heart candidates.

The covering fire stopped and we were ordered to begin our assault. The steep hill was dotted with loose granite and slippery with ice. Hidden silhouette targets popped up to our front and we pumped rifle fire into them. Clambering higher we reloaded, our stiff fingers fumbling with the clips. We reached the individual pits designated for our grenade throw and arced a wobbling flight of frags into the air. All but one. A trainee to my right had caught his throwing arm in his training rope. The live grenade had tumbled at his feet. He launched himself up and out of the pit to sprawl flat as the grenade boomed and covered us with dirt.

We moved upward. The hill had taken on the proportions of a mountain as we tried to "kill" another series of targets. Our leg muscles ached, our hearts pounded, and perspiration stung our eyes. We struggled higher — the river like a small creek far below — and flopped down exhausted. A scattered row of bayonet dummies were outlined on the crest of the hill. The order came to fix bayonets. Spitting cotton, we unsheathed our blades and clicked them in place.

"Charge!," the captain shouted. "Charge!" the sergeant bellowed, urging us forward. We pushed ourselves off the ground and stumbled toward the dummies in slow motion, the bayoneted rifles heavy in our hands. A few half-hearted thrusts at the rain swollen sandbags and we collapsed on the ground, gasping for breath and fumbling for our canteens.

The general arrived on the scene in his jeep. He didn't seem too pleased but he appeared to be a fatherly, forgiving man. He gave us a short pep talk, decreed an hour break before we began our 25 mile trek back to camp, and waved us a salute before driving off. By nightfall we still had five painful miles to go when someone sent some half-tracks out for us. Later, lathering up for a much-needed shower, it occurred to me how fortunate it was that no cameraman had been assigned to cover our exercise. If the footage had found its way to the Germans the rise in their morale might have lengthened the war by at least six months. ∎

*T*he enemy may have been waiting for us in Europe and the Pacific, but the roiling Deschutes became our real antagonist.

Illustration by Howard R. Simpson

Little Known Tales
from Oregon History

No. 69

ABC's
In One Room

By Karen Huntington

Country school teachers in the 1800s and early 1900s were among the most courageous pioneers in the history of the American West. The majority of them were young, single women. Teaching alone in one-room schoolhouses scattered in isolated locations, they suffered incredible hardships, yet they persevered, successfully bestowing powerful positive influences upon the communities they served.

What motivated these unsung heroes?

Teaching provided neither wealth nor a glamorous lifestyle. The average salary for a female country school teacher around the turn of the century was approximately $50 a month plus room and board. Some districts paid part of the earned salary in commodities such as yard goods, flour, or chickens. Various families in the community furnished the teacher's room and board. To avoid showing favorites or overtaxing anyone's budget, the teacher was moved frequently from household to household. Teachers often found themselves crammed in a tiny bed with several small children. Yet they remained, steadfast, determined to fulfill the obligations of their calling.

Although few other career opportunities were open to women at that time, those who chose to leave the comfort and security of home behind to accept teaching positions in country schools out West exhibited an unusually strong desire to control their own lives, uncharacteristic of women of their era. They were plucky, daring women. Some may have embarked on the venture thinking it would provide a romantic adventure, but the rugged life that awaited them was far from romantic.

Country school teachers had to be well organized and highly skilled in a variety of areas. Often lacking adequate textbooks and teaching tools, they taught reading, writing, arithmetic, geography, history, spelling, and music to all the students from first through eighth grade. Working alone in remote locations, teachers also had to serve as counselors, mediators, discipli-

Country school teachers must be regarded as the unsung heroes in the history of the American West.

narians, janitors, nurses, and protectors of their students. Teachers treated their students for everything from runny noses to broken bones, and many routinely patrolled the school grounds for wild predators and rattlesnakes. Parents expected teachers to be able to handle these responsibilities. A stalwart western parent once said, "If a teacher hasn't enough sense and know-how to kill a rattlesnake, she'd better go back where she came from."

At that time people in rural communities provided their own entertainment, and schoolhouses were the center of social activities. Those

little, old schoolhouses buzzed with Literary Society meetings, political debates, box socials, songfests, concerts, and holiday programs. Teacher's contracts often stipulated they have their students present at least two programs a year. Everyone in the community flocked to the schoolhouse to enjoy the plays, recitations, and musical programs performed by the students directed by their overworked teachers.

To accomplish all that was expected of them, country school teachers had to maintain strict discipline. Enterprising teachers incorporated

FAR LEFT: A country schoolteacher poses with her class in front of a one-room schoolhouse in Baker County.
Photo by Glass, Oregon Historical Society, #OrHi 36535

BELOW: This rustic schoolhouse served the tiny town of Wamic, located just northwest of Maupin in Wasco County, circa 1911.
Photo courtesy Keith Clark, Oregon Historical Society, #OrHi 75551

janitorial work into their discipline programs, assigning cleaning tasks the teacher was supposed to perform to students who disrupted the classroom. When necessary, they utilized dunce caps and liberally applied hickory rods. This met with the approval of parents and school boards.

In the book, *Whispers from Old Genesee and Echoes of the Salmon River,* John A. Platt wrote that during a young woman's interview for a teaching position in old Genesee, she was asked just one vital question: "What would you do if confronted with an obstreperous child?"

"I'd give him a licking!" she exclaimed.

Satisfied, the interviewer nodded. "You're hired."

Students quickly learned that education was important and disruptive behavior that interferred with the educational process would not be tolerated.

Country school teachers could freely implement any form of discipline they chose, but they had much less freedom in conducting their personal lives. In fact, there was no such thing as a private, personal life for a country school teacher. Everything the teacher said or did, whether on duty or not, was scrutinized by the community. Rural school administrations in the West tolerated nothing short of exemplary behavior from the teachers they employed. Depending upon the code of ethics of the individual community, teachers could be fired for inappropriate behavior, however minor, such as dancing, making an innocent slip of the tongue that offended an influential citizen, or merely befriending someone the rest of the community shunned. They had no job security, unlike tenured teachers today who are almost impossible to fire for any reason.

My grandmother, Edith Ward Killingsworth, left her home in Missouri in 1911, to teach in a remote one-room schoolhouse in Peola, Washington. She described her av-

Cascades East publisher, Geoff Hill, attended this country school in Sumpter, Oregon, from 1947 to 1952. One teacher taught grades one through eight in one room, while another teacher had a room of high school aged students. The lower, back portion of the building was used as a wintertime recess play area. The upper back was for Christmas programs, plays, and musical recitals. Photo courtesy Geoff Hill.

erage working day as grueling, but rewarding. Early each morning she rushed to school and lit a fire in the potbellied stove. Then she dusted and cleaned the building while she waited for her students to arrive on horseback, rosy cheeked and thoroughly chilled on cold winter mornings. Throughout the school day, she divided her time among the students, giving assignments and hearing recitations in all the subjects for every grade level. To ease her burden and maintain order, she assigned the older, more advanced students who finished their lessons ahead of schedule to tutor students in lower grades who needed extra help. She believed this interaction between students proved beneficial to all concerned. The younger students received the individualized instruction they needed, and the older students remained occupied and mentally stimulated, minimizing disruptions arising from idleness or boredom. Grandmother worked late into the evening, grading papers and planning lessons to make sure her eighth grade stu-

dents would be able to pass the proficiency tests required for graduation.

In those days, functional illiterates were not allowed to graduate from eighth grade. The statistics of our modern educational system are much less impressive. A study in 1982 revealed that 20% of adult Americans are functionally illiterate and in addition, another 34% are only marginally literate. In 1900, Iowa, Kansas, and Nebraska, predominantly rural in nature, boasted the highest literacy rates in the nation, surpassing urban areas in the east that invested more money in their educational systems.

In spite of the difficult circumstances, limited resources and lack of fixed curriculum, country school teachers did an amazing job. The high degree of success achieved by those brave country school teachers indicates they were motivated by a genuine sense of mission. Grandmother and her colleagues earned their keep. Their efforts greatly contributed to the taming and shaping of America. ■

The Queen Who Came To Visit

The intriguing story of how the steam launch "The African Queen," made famous in the movie of the same name, ended up in Central Oregon running excursions on the Deschutes.

By Don Burgderfer

In 1952 I saw a movie which has remained one of my all-time favorites. It was the film adaptation of a book by C.S. Forester called "The African Queen." Little did I dream, those 40 years ago, that the Queen and I would someday meet face-to-face in Central Oregon!

The whole saga of this amazing 80-year-old lady began in 1912, when a 30-foot long, eight-foot wide steam launch made of steel was fabricated in England for the British East Africa Railway Company.

The vessel was then transported by ship, rail, and truck to Lake Victoria and subsequently to Lake Albert. The boat was quite likely pre-fabricated in smaller sections in England and then assembled at the Lake Albert destination.

Records indicate that the vessel was originally named the S/L (steam launch) Livingstone (after the famous African explorer). It was used primarily as a work boat and as a conveyance for tourists and hunters. It was first powered by a steam engine and later on by a 10-horse-power diesel engine.

In 1951, film producer Sam

Spiegel hired director John Huston to bring the Forester book to life. They obtained Katherine Hepburn to play Rosie Sayer, the sister of missionary Samuel Sayer (Robert Morley); and for the grim Canadian operator of the African Queen (Charlie Allnut), they made the brilliant and unforgettable choice of Humphrey Bogart. Hepburn had apparently never been to Africa, wanted to see it, and insisted the filming be done there!

Whether it was because Kate wanted to go to Africa or not, Spiegel did decide to do a great deal of the production in Africa, and the general locations were (as they were known then) the Belgian Congo and the British Protectorate of Uganda. The first film camp was at Biondo, on the Ruiki River, a tributary of the Congo River. Other scenes were filmed at Lake Albert in Uganda and at studios in England. The story is set in September, 1914, early WWI days, and Rose and brother Samuel are running a mission in Africa. German soldiers pass by the mission, during which time Samuel is beaten, and the village is destroyed. He subsequently sickens and dies. Rose is left alone, and the Germans are likely to return. But, at this time, a most unlikely savior arrives in the form of a drunken supply boat operator, one Charlie Allnut. Sparks are inevitable between the prim, religious English woman and the uncouth river rat. But, retreat from the returning Germans is the best choice for both; so Samuel is buried, and Rose chugs off down the uncertain river with Charlie, his gin supply, and the grimy African Queen.

The trip down the river is sometimes serene and sometimes harrowing; but patriotic Rose, a stubborn Englishwoman to the core, decides that the African Queen will become the instrument of destruction of the Princess Louise, a German gunboat on the lake at then end of the river. You know the rest. But, I can assure you that the film company did not really destroy our beloved African Queen to effect the end of the story. The Queen still lives!

In 1951, according to James Hendricks, present owner of the Queen, director John Huston told his assistant art director, John Hoesli, to find a boat that resembled the one described in Forester's book. Hoesli found such a boat at Lake Albert, and the S/L Livingstone was transformed into the African Queen.

When Hoesli first saw the boat, the original steam engine and boiler had been removed and

replaced by a 10-HP diesel. He commissioned a firm in Nairobi to install a fake boiler and steam engine for the movie so the boat would look like the one described in the book. At Hoesli's direction the boat was painted with mud to make her old and and rusty looking, as per the book description. During the movie, the steam boiler was actually driving the steam engine, but it was the diesel engine which was really propelling the boat!

While based at the Biondo location on the Ruiki River, the Queen developed a leak one night and sank. Heavy equipment aboard was removed and the vessel was refloated, to the relief of all. After the filming at Biondo was completed, the ship was taken back to Lake Albert and up the Victoria Nile, where many of the other river scenes were filmed.

You probably well remember the episode where the boat is hopelessly trapped in a maze of reeds, then rains come and the Queen floats free of its prison and gains access to the lake which was so close but was unseen. These scenes were filmed at the mouth of the Nile where it empties into Lake Albert. (In the movie, no name was given to the lake, and the rivers were given fictitious names.)

Actually, there was a second African Queen used during the filming, but this was just a partial mock-up built on a raft. It featured basically the back seat/tiller position and the spot near the boiler where Bogie stood and "gave it a kick in the slats" now and then. The need for such a mock-up was an absolute necessity. The motion picture camera being used was quite large; supplemental lighting was necessary (as is usual in filming); and lots of various crew members were always needed in close vicinity. Trying to do all this close-up work on the actual Queen would have been an impossibility. Interestingly enough, whenever it had to appear that this mock-up of the Queen was moving, the raft was towed by the real African Queen or another boat. Thus, the Queen was a real working member of the crew, not just a celebrity. But, this was nothing new; the African Queen had been a work boat all its life.

The actual boat was not used in the scenes where the African Queen was required to travel over dangerous river falls. Half-size models (with half-size model people) had been constructed to be guided through the falls by wires. Also, the underwater scenes (fixing the broken propeller, etc.) and Bogie's famous towing scenes were not made in Africa at all. They were filmed at a tank in London. This was because personnel were not allowed into the waters in Africa due to the presence of a life threatening, water-borne parasite.

As they say, "fame is fleeting." After movie production ended, the fake boiler and steam engine were removed from the diesel-powered boat and it remained a work boat on Lake Albert for the next 16 years.

In November, 1967, Mr. Fred Reeve of San Francisco learned from a foreign news service item that the African Queen was for sale. Reeve immediately flew to Nairobi, but he was too late. The old girl had been auctioned off for $400. Reeve contacted the buyer and offered him $730 plus a replacement boat. The deal was struck and he obtained his prize!

In 1968, the Queen arrived at San Francisco. Reeve restored the vessel, retaining its mock-up steam plant. (Prior to auction, the British East Africa Railway Company had removed the functional diesel engine and had installed a fake boiler, so the Queen was essentially without any propulsion system at the time Reeve bought it.) At one time Reeve sailed the boat across San Francisco Bay, but he had to use an outboard motor for propulsion. The results of this voyage were reported as being "dismal."

Reeve didn't retain ownership of the Queen very long. Sometime near the autumn of 1968, Hal Bailey of Eugene, Oregon, noticed a one-paragraph item in his city's Eugene Register-Guard that the Queen was for sale. He located the boat at San Rafael, California, bought it, and had it shipped to Eugene on one of his own trucks. Upon close examination of the vessel, he discovered the awful truth. He was dismayed to find that the "steam plant" was merely a mock-up (courtesy of the British East Africa Railway Company). But, what Hal had really wanted was a genuine steam-driven boat, and he immediately set to work finding serviceable steam components for his prize.

Bailey found a suitable steam engine attached to an old cider press in Ashland, Oregon. He then found an ASME-code boiler at a tree nursery in Portland. Both pieces of equipment had been in storage for years, but were found to be in good, serviceable condition. They were incorporated into the old boat and did, in fact, render much good service.

The Central Oregon Connection

Hal Bailey was one of the original investors in the Sunriver development project south of Bend. He thought it would be nice to bring the African Queen to Central Oregon and offer tourist rides on a renowned, one-of-a-kind boat. In 1969, the African Queen was placed into the Deschutes River at the Sunriver

The African Queen returns to the Sunriver Marina after a trip on the Deschutes River in the fall of 1971. Photo by Don Burgderfer

Marina and provided river excursions to nostalgic tourists through 1971. It was Bailey's old apple-cider engine that powered the boat during its stay at Sunriver. And, that old steam plant never gave a bit of trouble!

In 1970, even Charles Kuralt came to Sunriver to do a story about the African Queen. Quality old movie stars always have a hold on the media.

While at Sunriver, the African Queen was usually piloted by Peter McCook, whose father, Anson, was manager of the Sunriver airport at the time. The boat took passengers several miles downstream to the Benham Falls area and then turned around and slowly chugged back upstream to the marina. Or sometimes it went upstream first then leisurely returned with the current.

In a 1988 interview, the elder McCook reported that the African Queen was in pristine condition when it was at Sunriver, thanks to Hal Bailey's efforts. Anson said, "It handled well in the river. But, it was a slow trip coming back from Benham Falls against the current. He said he really enjoyed sitting there and listening to the old steam engine chugging away. His observation betrays a fascination evidenced by a lot of people toward the old steam engines of yesteryear.

I talked to Peter McCook, the tillerman on the African Queen while it was at Sunriver. Peter is now a metals broker in Irvine, California. His is a high-pressure, modern-age job in current society. But, it was obvious that Peter relished reliving some of his fond memories of that years-ago, more laid-back life of piloting the African Queen on the Deschutes River.

In the 1969 Sunriver lifestyle, Peter was a shirtless, jeans-clad youth who was working at a very low profile job at Sunriver Marina. As he put it, "In those days, we had maybe three canoes to rent." Into this laid-back life was thrust an unexpected celebrity: the African Queen. He was designated to be the tillerman (pilot) of the vessel. As

Peter related to me, "It took two people to run the Queen, a tillerman and a boilerman." Another young man who worked at the marina, Scott Ferguson, was selected to be the boilerman. Sometimes, to relieve boredom, Peter said he and Scott would switch jobs. Even Bogie had to have Katherine Hepburn handle the tiller while he kicked and coaxed the old steam engine.

Peter McCook told me the charges for rides were pretty nominal - "Maybe around three dollars or so." He commented it was indeed a very slow trip back upriver whenever they went down to Benham Falls. And how did they keep that good old boiler stoked? Peter said that once a week he and Scott would go into the woods in the lower part of Sunriver where there was plenty of down, dead and dry timber. They would cut this stuff up, bring it back to the Sunriver marina, split it, and stack it in a woodpile they maintained. Every night Scott or Peter would stoke the Queen's boiler so that a good head of steam could be developed quickly the next morning when the boiler was again stoked.

Echoing his father's sentiments, Peter told me the old cider press engine had a great sound to it. "However," he added, "it also had a very loud steam whistle. Local environmentalists used to get upset because they felt the loud shrieks possibly disturbed ospreys and other birds nesting along the river."

Peter said they usually took six or seven people on their river tours. I asked him if they ever had any particular problems with the vessel. Said Peter, "It was a fun old boat. We never had any problems with the Queen on the river. The only problem was when Scott or I would forget to stoke the boiler at night; next morning, no steam!" Peter added, "The engine was quite low-tech and very simple to operate." "All in all," he reminisced, "that was a fun way to spend a summer!"

I somehow felt that Peter, now enmeshed in his high-pressure, modern-world vocation of metals

arbitrage, looked with great wistfulness upon his youthful job of piloting the African Queen along the peaceful, meandering Deschutes River of Central Oregon. He clearly relished reliving those experiences. Alas, Peter, we all had our halycon days of youth, and we share with you the memories of same, though few of us can count a true Queen amongst our past lives.

Hal Bailey, the Queen's owner during the Sunriver years, apparently did take a ride on her now and then. He was once quoted as saying, "When you hold the Queen's tiller in your hand and go ka-thunk, ka-thunk, ka-thunk up the river, it's just something else and a half!" Just another steam engine nut, we might assume. But, don't they have fun!

Unfortunately for Central Oregon, after the 1971 boating season Hal Bailey removed the African Queen from Sunriver and began exhibiting it in the national boat show circuit. It was, of course, a major attraction. One would have thought that Kate and Bogie were still aboard the old work boat!

After the middle seventies the Queen fell into disuse. In 1982 it was purchased by James W. Hendricks for $65,000 (a far cry from the $730 of 1967!). Hal Bailey, now of Punta Gorda, Florida, has visited the Queen several times since selling it to Hendricks. When it is not on tour, the boat resides at the Holiday Inn Harbor, Key Largo, Florida.

Since being acquired by Hendricks, the Queen has been all around the United States and has, literally, been all around the world. It has a specially-made boat trailer upon which it travels by road, ferry, rail, or steamship, as conditions warrant.

James Hendricks prides himself on taking good care of the African Queen, regarding it as a historical treasure that should be preserved and shared with the public. We do not, as a collective American Republic, treat our movie momentos lightly!

In May of 1990, Hendricks attempted to take the little boat across the English Channel as part of the Dunkirk Commemoration activities, but mechanical difficulties aborted the voyage after a number of hours. Later that June, with the mechanical difficulties corrected, the Queen successfully made the trip in about four-and-a-half hours from Dover to Calais. Hendricks and his hearty crew were then royally treated by the French at Calais Harbor.

Prior to the Channel attempt, Hal Bailey's old apple cider steam plant (which served admirably on the Deschutes River) had been removed and a new boiler and steam engine installed. These were faithful replicas of 1880's English steam launch power plants, though the boiler was fabricated in Los Angeles according to old-time specifications.

The African Queen is not to be ignored, even to this day. As recently as May 22, 1992, the vessel was still generating news items. AP reported that some tourist taking a picture of the boat at his Holiday Inn moorage at Key Largo accidentally bumped an electrical switch on the dock's boat lift mechanism. Unfortunately, only the bow of the Queen was attached to the lift at the time and as the bow was lifted, the stern sank and pulled the grand old boat under. So once again, as at the Ruiki River in 1951, the Queen had to be rescued from a watery grave and put back into commission.

At last report, the African Queen was still engaged in taking tourists on excursions, as it has off and on for the past 80 years. Its steam engine still happily goes ka-thunk, ka-thunk, ka-thunk, as a good steam engine should. And Charlie and Rosie, if they could be there, would surely have a blast! ∎

ACKNOWLEDGEMENTS: My great thanks to Jim Hendricks, present owner of the African Queen, and to Mrs. Anson (Judy) McCook and Peter McCook, who, in their own ways, have been very, very close to that grand old hulk of a steam boat.

HOT LAKES
Continued from page 73

range, more exotic plans, were to build a large greenhouse, capitalizing on the warmth and humidity of the steaming waters, and grow English cucumbers and mushrooms to ship fresh all year long. Randolph Griffith worked with Boise State University on a project to grow both tropical and warm water game fish such as cats and bass in pay-to-fish ponds. Ornamental fish raised in water with a high mineral content have a much deeper hue and command premium prices in the national wholesale market. Creamy petaled lilies, already growing thick in the ponds surrounding the hotel, were to be enhanced and harvested for an existing market.

There seemed to be no limit to the potential for Hot Lake's mineral water, hot and gushing from the earth at 1,780 gallons per minute, or two and a half million gallons per day.

The big – and immediate – plan was for a 23-acre RV development with 100 sites, three hot mineral pools at varying temperatures, a laundromat, restaurant, and grocery store. The land was cleared and leveled in 1987 with the help of an Oregon EDD-guaranteed loan and a $100,000 grant from the Bureau of Indian Affairs, garnered because the senior Griffith is a member of the South Dakota Ogalalla tribe. After the park opened in May 1989, the story took a twist.

More money was needed, and more investors sought for the nearly finished project. One of the investors, a retired military doctor and personal acquaintance of Dr. Griffith, invested heavily in the venture and was rewarded by having the RV park entrance named for him: General Sheldon Bronton Boulevard. But the additional funds could not reverse the downward financial spiral, and it went into receivership in 1990. The RV park property, separated from the Hotel and its 300-plus acre grounds, is managed by a firm out of Vancouver, Washington, for the lenders who foreclosed. The park remains open nine months of the year in a beautiful setting ringed by mountains and marshes alive with ducks, geese, and birds. Deer graze on the sage-covered hills stretching over to become part of the Ladd Canyon which caused the pioneers so much grief as they labored into the valley.

There seemed to be no limit to the potential for Hot Lake's mineral water, hot and gushing from the earth.

A quarter mile away sits the grand old Hot Lake Hotel, overlooking the steaming grounds like a grand dame at court from another time. The doors closed again in 1991 and the bankruptcy courts have ordered it sold. Ironically, the realtor who has the listing is one of the partners in the failed western nightclub venture ending in 1977. The paint is weathered, the rain pours through the leaking roof along with the pigeons which flap and whir through the upper floors, sounding like yesterday's residents whispering reminiscences, or perhaps like the ghosts who have long traveled the vast halls. According to some who have recently entered the building, the fixtures are gone, the walls and restrooms have been stripped of the inlaid marble and intricate handiwork created in a time long ago when there was pride of workmanship and money to pay for it.

Despite the damage, the structure, grounds, and waters give the visitor a sense of the past splendor and if one listens carefully, the music and laughter, the bustle and excitement can still be heard in the empty halls. Perhaps in 1993 as the Oregon Trail celebrates its 150-year mark, the right combination of interests and resources can heal and bring back to life this wonderful, natural asset so that it, in turn, can once again be a Northwest destination to heal and enjoy. ∎

The Hot Lake RV Park is located eight miles south of LaGrande off Interstate 84 at Exit 268.

The Rise & Fall

In its glory days, Eastern Oregon's Hot Lake Hote

LEFT: Hot Lake at the peak of its splendor. The masonry structure at the left end is the Union Pacific's addition at the turn of the century; the frame structures at the right were the original "town under one roof," built in the 1890s. Note the tiny circular spring house at the far right. The original cement base withstood the "great fire," was reroofed, and was used as a sauna until the 1970s. Photo by Richardson, *Oregon Journal*, Oregon Historical Society, #OrHi 39576

RIGHT: Inside the spring house, the wooden "fence" has since been replaced by a rock structure. One can look down and watch the hot springs bubble from the earth. Oregon Historical Society, OrHi #15881

By Jan Minarik-Holt

For centuries, man has "taken the waters" at Hot Lake, a picturesque mineral pool bubbling out of the earth's core to form a steaming lake eight miles south of LaGrande in the Grand Rhonde Valley of Northeastern Oregon.

The earliest man came to winter. The Yakima, Nez Perce, Umatilla, and some lesser tribes made this a neutral area where wounds of the heart healed while the warm mineral waters soothed and healed wounds of the body. Their horses grazed on grass kept green by the constant temperature of the earth, regardless of the depth of the snow pack or the severity of the winter.

In 1812, the first white man stumbled across the steaming sulphuric waters. Robert Stewart, a member of the Wilson Hunt Price expedition, described the discovery in his journal and wrote of thousands of shed elk antlers covering the

ground for a half mile in every direction. The long growing season made the fertile area a favorite for wildlife as well as for man, as attested to in Washington Irving's 1836 *Astoria*:

> "Emerging from the chain of Blue Mountains, they descended upon a vast plain... they passed close to the skirts of the hills, a great pool of water 300 yards in circumference, fed by a sulphur spring boiling up in one corner... The vapor from this pool was extremely noisome, and tainted the air for a considerable distance. The place was much frequented by elk, which were found in considerable numbers in the adjacent mountain, and their horns, shed in the springtime, were stewed in every direction around the pond."

The emigrants struggling west over the Oregon Trail sought out the mecca as a resting area after descending Ladd Canyon, one of the most rigorous challenges on the long trip. The little spur road leading to the Oregon Trail is still visible along the base of the canyon wall south of the present day structures.

In 1864, an enterprising Californian, Sam Newhart, took claim to the area and developed it into the "Town Under One Roof," the world's first covered shopping mall. The blacksmith shop still stands; the post office kept its mark until the 1930s.

LEFT: The lobby of the Hot Lake Hotel, circa 1930, was where one could buy train tickets or post mail. Imagine 1,200 guests per day strolling through this spacious lobby! The carpeting is still in use.
Oregon Historical Society, OrHi #15886

RIGHT: Thousands of guests once filled the rocking chairs on this sun porch. Today, this room stores the oak filing cabinets still filled with records of the patients who took the waters at Hot Lake, or who spent their waning years in the hotel after its conversion to a nursing home.
Oregon Historical Society, OrHi #15882

There was also a dance hall, barber shop, candy store, drug store, garden shop, and of course, the baths. Spas were the rage worldwide during the late 1800s and early 1900s.

Viewing Hot Lake as an exciting and profitable destination, the Union Pacific Railroad purchased the resort about the turn of the century. The railroad did not lay its track to run in a straight line east across the valley floor toward what would become its most famous resort at Sun Valley, Idaho. Rather the steel rails curve across the lush Grande Rhonde Valley and sweep in front of Hot Lake to the little depot where the genteel passengers disembarked and later bought return tickets to their homes all over the country.

Under the Oregon Railroad and Navigation Company flag, the railroad built a spacious three-story brick building over a several-year period, costing 500,000 sound dollars. The third floor was designed as a sanitarium and nursing school. Today, this mammoth brick annex housing the sanitarium is all that stands after a raging Sunday fire in 1934 took the original wooden struc-

tures — the original "Town Under One Roof." The operating room is still intact, the huge viewing window staring blankly at the stark white room, its total surface area covered with smooth, one-inch ceramic tiles. The imported marble and porcelain fixtures are in place; the silver-coated sterilizers stand at attention, waiting to be put into service. Bed pans litter the shelves in the nurses' stations next to stacks of blank clipboards. The solid marble urinal in the doctors' bathroom, imported from Italy, rests idly under a blanket of dust, plaster crumbs, and pigeon feathers.

The Glory Days

Shortly after its completion in 1900, the sanitarium and medical school were put under the apt management of Dr. William Phy, a skilled surgeon. Dr. Phy, as manager and Chief of Medicine, led Hot Lake Hotel to world-wide eminence as the sister school of the famed Mayo Clinic of Minnesota. The Mayo brothers, close friends of Dr. Phy, visited the hotel many times during his tenure.

The "Mayo Clinic of the West" was on the leading edge in developing and evaluating new medical technology. Radiation therapy was one of

the innovations, and the x-ray machine used by Dr. Phy and his aides is still lodged next to his office, ready to start up at the flip of a switch. This machine, with its electric static generator, predates the one on display at the Smithsonian Museum.

Arthritis, tuberculosis, alcoholism, and venereal diseases, especially syphilis, were treated at the clinic. Dr. Phy put to use the sulphuric waters flowing from the earth at 186°F, tempered for the repeated baths that he believed the syphilis organism could not withstand.

From the turn of the century through the roaring twenties were glory days for Hot Lake Resort. While the preeminent Dr. Phy successfully continued to research, teach and treat at the medical school, the resort became the cultural center for Eastern Oregon. As many as 1,200 guests each day lounged in wicker settees, played shuffleboard under the hanging ferns, shopped, danced, dined, and took the waters.

The Dark Years

Bleakness descended with the great depression. In 1932 Dr. Phy "took a chill" after falling into the Columbia River on a duck hunting trip at The Dalles with his companions, the Mayo brothers, and subsequently died. His physician son, Mark, followed him in death two years later. The resort floundered under new owners and the constantly changing management as the Union Pacific gradually divested its ownership and support. Through the dark years the third floor continued to house the hospital for the Grand Rhonde Valley.

During World War II, a pilots' school was garrisoned in the hotel and the medical school became a nurses' training center. This convenient arrangement was the cause of many romantic attachments and subsequent marriages.

At the close of the war, Dr. Roth, a Washington State College professor, bought the entire complex and converted it to a nursing home, thus changing Hot Lake's destiny for the next 30 years.

Although the nursing home was successful, Hot Lake lost its allure. It now reeked of old age and sickness; gone was the magic of lights and music, the glittering affluence, the daring pilots and young nurses. The huge structure loomed empty, its windows dark except for part of the upper floors.

Dr. Roth's tenure ended and the nursing home closed in 1974. Those who believe in the ghost stories say this is when the nocturnal visits of piano playing and screams began. This is also when the restaurant and country western night club opened which many residents remember as a great place to dine, listen to top-name western singers then take a dip in the hot mineral pool outside. But Eastern Oregon didn't have the population to carry the venture, and the doors closed and the windows darkened in 1977. Rooms were emptied of furniture, drapes, carpet, even the brass plates were pulled off the doors. The plumbing, which had coursed hot water through the entire structure for three quarters of a century was drained for the first time, allowing cold and damp to seep into the grand old building. Plaster fell in crumbling chunks, pipes froze and burst, hardwood floors buckled and twisted. The leaking roof let in rain and snow; then, in final despair, allowed in pigeons to wander the vast halls. Trapped, they died and lay mute in feathery heaps in the stairwells. The low point of Hot Lake's existence came when shareholders met to consider razing the structure and selling the bricks for ten cents each.

Renovation Attempts

In 1983, another physician stepped in to play a hand in the fate of Hot Lake Hotel. Dr. Lyle Griffith, a LaGrande resident and long-time shareholder, bought out the others and took steps to stop the deterioration of the historical resort, and even breathe new life into it. His son and wife, Randolph and Marie Griffith, moved in to help with the grand dream and reorganized as Hot Lake Company.

Emergency repairs were made to the roof. Some renovations were completed but were slow and costly under codes much different from those adhered to by Union Pacific in 1900. Spacious, claw-foot tubs were moved from the nursing home suites to a renovated ground floor room for mineral soaks adjacent to a new cedar-lined sauna. The great lounge, where once the long-skirted damsels of society directed the porters with luggage, hosted laser tag for kids while their parents soaked.

The Griffiths' plans included a bed and breakfast on the second floor where the suites were already plumbed and enhanced with closets, mantle facades, curved glass windows, and grand views of the mountains and valley. Their long-

Continued on page 69

Despite the damage, the visitor will sense the past splendor and if one listens carefully, the music and laughter, the bustle and excitement can still be heard in the empty halls.

Weeds grow unchecked, the roof leaks, and the elegant historic hotel is ordered sold by bankruptcy court.
Photo courtesy of Jan Minarik-Holt

The Fort That Vanished

— Bend's Claim to Film and Fortune —

By Don Burgderfer

Western movies were extremely popular in the 1950s, but after a while it did seem like the same MGM back-lot and Monument Valley settings that so often appeared were getting a little jaded. Fresh western vistas were needed, and the film production companies sent scouts all around the west to find them. They would, of course, have had to be quite blind not to notice the abundance and striking variety of raw scenery available in Central Oregon.

But, more than just new scenery was needed. A stockade fort was also a requirement for one of the films to be produced in the Bend area. In 1955, a site for the "fort" was located on a butte above Benham Falls on the Deschutes River. *(See the story on page 4.)* The construction project was a joint venture that was initiated by Byrna Productions, Inc., of Hollywood, California. One of the major stockholders of that firm was actor Kirk Douglas.

Other parties were involved in this project. Since Forest Service land was involved, a special-use permit had to be obtained from the Deschutes National Forest. An especially important local partner in the enterprise was the Bend Chamber of Commerce, because the undertaking had important economic implications for the growing town of Bend.

Logs and lumber for the stockade were mostly provided by Lelco and Brooks-Scanlon. Local people were hired to do the construction work, and total cost of the stockade was about $30,000. Mean-

Fresh western vistas were needed, and the film production companies sent scouts all around the west to find them. They would have been blind not to notice the abundance and variety of raw scenery available in Central Oregon.

while, the USFS and Deschutes County assisted in building roads to the location.

Local Bend citizens had their own favorite names for the new movie set: Chamber of Commerce Fort, Deschutes Fort, and Movie Fort. The Bend *Bulletin* finally suggested "Fort Benham" as an appropriate name, and it stuck.

In 1955, the movie "The Indian Fighter" was filmed at the fort by Byrna Productions. It starred (naturally) Kirk Douglas and supporting cast included Elsa Martinelli, Lon Chaney Jr., and Walter Matthau.

In 1957, parts of "Oregon Passage" were filmed at Fort Benham. It starred John Ericson and Lola Albright. Disney Studios took notice of the Fort Benham area in 1958 and used it in the filming of "Tonka" (subsequently retitled "A Horse Named Comanche.") Sal Mineo and a horse were the stars of that film.

By the turn of the decade, Richard

Boone's popular "Have Gun, Will Travel" series had found its way to Central Oregon, and no less than six episodes were filmed in the Fort Benham area and also near Vandervert Ranch. Some of the period furniture used in the interior scenes at the stockade had been borrowed from Bend's Pilot Butte Inn. At one point, someone in the Boone party accidentally dropped a sixgun into the Deschutes River from the old General Patch Bridge. Skindivers were used to retrieve the firearm, and someone in the cast undoubtedly had a *very* red face over that affair!

The summer of 1962 presaged the approaching decline of Fort Benham. Some young anglers on the river below the butte let a campfire get away from them. The roaring inferno raced uphill toward the fort, and the Forest Service went to work.

According to forester Andy Coray, who was involved in the firefighting effort, retardant bombers were called out and their major mission was to "save Fort Benham!" And they did save it, even to the extent of dropping retardant directly on the fort. (The result was a pink fort until the next rains came.) The areas around the fort were quite blackened before the conflagration could be finally controlled. And, sadly, the scenic filming value of the surrounding area had been completely devastated for years to come by the fire.

Other things had been happening at the fort. Vandals were beginning to take their toll on the premises, and fires had even been set in some of the interior

The exterior view of the entrance into the Fort Benham stockade. The U.S. Forest Service planted pine trees all across this area after the fort was demolished in 1963. INSET: The inside view of the Fort Benham stockade entrance. The buildings seen here were used for filming interior scenes, sometimes with period furniture borrowed from the Pilot Butte Inn. Photos courtesy of Don Burgderfer

structures. But, there was worse news. When the stockade was originally constructed, untreated pine logs had simply been placed into the ground. Anyone who has built a fence using untreated pine posts knows what happens. Within just a few years the underground portions of the posts simply rot away and crumble. And, so it was with Fort Benham's stockade.

Officials of the USFS Bend Ranger District and the Bend Chamber of Commerce inspected the site in early 1963 and recommended to the Chamber that the fort be razed. The place was starting to topple over and was becoming a growing

hazard to anyone who visited there. According to Ray Bennett, the Bend District Ranger at the time, repair costs to the rotting structure would have been exhorbitant. In addition, because of the previous year's fire, the motion picture value of the site was nil. For the last couple of years the USFS had been pressing the Chamber to get rid of the fort. Now it was time to act. In March, 1963, it was announced that Fort Benham would be demolished.

A local Bend businessman, Lyle Sabin, was awarded the contract to demolish what was left of Fort Benham. Apparently, a great amount of the sal-

vage material from there was sold for firewood. Later, the Forest Service went in and planted trees over the then barren site. In addition, all of the old vehicle roads into the area have now been blocked off by the Bend Ranger District.

Through the years, Fort Benham served as a considerable tourist attraction because of its national publicity as a motion picture site. Over the eight years it existed, it was estimated to have brought an influx of well over a million dollars into the Bend community. By golly, that's not too shabby a return for a $30,000 investment! ■

No. 73

Prineville Hotels Made History

Pistol shoot-outs, raging fires, smallpox epidemics, and skinny-dipping cowboys account for a few of the reasons the hotels in Prineville enjoyed such a colorful past.

By David Braly

First, chains dragging on the floor ... Later, a burst of pistol shots ... A short time after that, a man screaming. With so much noise coming up from the lobby, guests in a certain Prineville hotel one night in March 1882 didn't get much sleep.

Deputies had been holding a shackled prisoner in the lobby. He had murdered two neighbors in a property dispute and they planned to take him to The Dalles for trial. One deputy reported later:

"At about 5 o'clock in the morning, as I was sitting at the stove with my back to the front door, the door was suddenly opened and I was caught and thrown backward on the floor and firmly held, while my eyes were blinded. Immediately a pistol was fired rapidly five or six times ... [Later] I went to [the prisoner] and found him dead. I looked around and a masked man stood at each door, warning by omi-

The Hotel Oregon (1901-1917) was originally the Poindexter Hotel. Prineville residents believed that a fatal epidemic began in its dining room.
Photo courtesy Crook County Historical Society #853

The Jackson House (1876-1922) was also known as the Culver Hotel and the Old Prineville Hotel. The vigilantes who ruled Central Oregon for two years made their first appearance here.
Photo courtesy Crook County Historical Society, #865

nous signs for no one to undertake to leave the room."

These men, Prineville vigilantes, also grabbed an innocent man in the hotel who had worked on the murderer's ranch. They dragged him to death behind a horse and hanged him from the Crooked River bridge.

The hotel, the Jackson House, was located near the corner of Third and Main Streets. The Ochoco Inn and Cinnabar complex occupies the site today. One or another hostelry has stood on the "hospitality block" for almost 120 years.

Monroe Hodges built Prineville's first hotel a block from there. When he arrived in 1871, the hamlet's founder, Barney Prine, owned a cabin which served as a blacksmith shop and saloon. Hodges bought Prine's cabin and squatting rights for $25 and a horse. He then filed an 80-acre homestead claim and platted the town of Prineville. He built the Hodges Hotel later that year at the northwest corner of East Second and Main. Larkin ("Doc") Vanderpool used one room as a drugstore. Riders from The Dalles carried mail for Prineville to the hotel, and one of Hodges's sons distributed it.

Oliver P. Jackson built Prineville's second hotel in 1876 and managed it until 1880, when A. B. Culver took over. One account calls it the Culver Hotel, but people generally called it the Jackson House until it was renamed the Old Prineville Hotel. It was the first "hospitality block" and the place where the vigilantes surfaced that cold winter night in 1882.

Meanwhile, Hodges had sold his hotel. Dan Richards became operator of the renamed Occidental Hotel in 1880. The night of November 10, 1883, a fire broke out in the Occidental's kitchen. It spread swiftly through the rooms. Despite firefighters's efforts, soon the whole building and neighboring businesses became engulfed. The fire destroyed all the principal buildings on the west side of Main Street.

The richest man in Central Oregon was Ben Allen. He was the first rancher here to introduce sheep and Jersey cattle and in 1887 started the First National Bank of Prineville. And, at some point, the big-jawed rancher bought the Jackson House. Allen hired two Chinese brothers to manage it, Ah Doon and Moy Doon.

The first Chinese man to enter Prineville had been stoned. Residents tolerated Ah Doon because he was an excellent cook. A delegation of local cattlemen went to Allen's office and demanded that he fire his Chinese help. Allen said that employing them was good business, then changed the subject.

Later, Ah Doon took a stage to The Dalles on his way to buy merchandise in San Francisco. Not far from Prineville, four masked riders ordered the stage driver to pull up. When he stopped, three of the masked men dismounted, threw open the door, and dragged out Ah Doon. They cut off his queue, then warned him to never return to Prineville or he would be killed.

Ah Doon was furious, but not intimidated. After buying his merchandise in California, he returned. For a while, he owned the town's only restaurant. Prineville soon had a Chinatown.

Stable hand Perry Poindexter knew opportunity when he saw it. About 1888, Poindexter opened a new restaurant which advertised "absolutely no Chinese cooking" and "white waiters." He prospered. And, in 1902, he opened the Poindexter Hotel. Located on the east side of Main between Second and Third Streets, the handsome two-story hotel rivaled or surpassed the Old Prineville (formerly Jackson) Hotel.

In April 1903, a man arrived at the Poindexter, ate a meal in its dining room, and rented a room for the night. He left town the following morning. By then the two waitresses who'd served him had fallen sick. A doctor diagnosed smallpox.

Everyone assumed the stranger had brought it. No one knows what happened to him. The incubation period for smallpox argues for another source, but the Poindexter does appear to have been the flashpoint for the smallpox.

The disease spread from the Poindexter through town. Local authorities cut off Prineville from the world for six weeks. Volunteer guards occupied the roads to stop people from entering or leaving town. The marshal ordered that anyone who walked in town had to stay in the middle of the streets. Doctors vaccinated the children *en masse*. Officials then told parents to keep their children home. To prevent germs on the dead from escaping, they wrapped the coffins in sheets soaked in

The Hotel Prineville (1912-1922)
was said to be the finest hostelry east of the Cascades.
Made of native red stone, the contractor who built it said that it
was "fireproof" and the owner made the mistake of believing him.
Photo courtesy Crook County Historical Society

The lobby would have a marble counter, Circassian walnut woodwork, "ivory" side walls, and a frescoed ceiling. The bar and cardroom would be finished in oak.

formaldehyde. They buried these strange coffins in a special graveyard.

The Poindexter later became the Hotel Oregon. On November 22, 1917, a fire started in a confectionary next door and spread to the hotel. Two women ran through the halls waking sleeping guests. Everyone escaped, but the fire destroyed the Hotel Oregon and nearby buildings. The hotel owners decided not to rebuild.

Mrs. C. E. McDowell came into possession of the Old Prineville Hotel (formerly the Jackson House). She moved the wooden building to the east end of the block and made it an annex for a big new 50-room Hotel Prineville built of native red stone. The contractor assured her it would be fireproof. The new hotel dwarfed its competition.

"The Hotel Prineville is going to have a lobby and bar made of tile and marble that will be the finest east of the Cascades," observed a local newspaper shortly before the hotel opened in 1912.

The article went on to describe the facilities in detail, from the vitreous hexagon tile to the dark blue vein Alaska marble baseboard around each room. The lobby would have a marble counter, Circassian walnut woodwork, "ivory" side walls, and a frescoed ceiling. The bar and cardroom would be finished in oak.

Five years after the Hotel Oregon fire,

a few minutes before midnight on May 31, 1922, a fire broke out in a condemned ten-room schoolhouse which had been moved to Fourth and Belknap. A strong wind carried burning shingles to the Old Prineville Hotel annex and from there to the Hotel Prineville.

Firemen tried valiantly to save it. The "fireproof" hotel was destroyed in less than half an hour.

Aside from destroying the hotel, old hotel, school building, livery stables, two hardware stores, pool hall, grocery store, and big merchantile, the wind-whipped inferno quickly involved numerous other Prineville offices and businesses. City officials decided dynamite offered their only hope. They exploded it on Main between Fourth and Fifth Streets and at about 7 am, they finally brought the fire under control.

Mrs. McDowell had turned down a $50,000 offer for her magnificent hotel only a week earlier. On the grim, smoky morning of June 1, she stood in front of the bank, looking across the street at the rubble that had been the finest hotel east of the Cascades, tears streaming down her face. Promised that her building was fireproof, she'd saved money by not insuring it.

The fire destroyed $350,000 worth of property, the hotel accounting for $80,000 of this. City and fire officials blamed arson and Mayor Will Wurzeiler offered a

The Ochoco Inn (1923-1966) was for many years the center of community activity in Prineville. Today, its fountain, hidden here by the telephone pole, stands in front of the Crook County courthouse. Photo courtesy Crook County Historical Society #828-1

$1,200 reward. Others believed a defective flue had caused the fire. The actual cause remains a mystery.

In September, the directors of the Prineville Hotel Company revealed plans for another hotel on the site. With an appearance inspired by Spanish California architecture, it would be the biggest hotel yet, 64 rooms above a huge lobby, a dining room, and eight stores which would be leased out. It would meaure 120 x 240 feet and be "as near to fireproof as it is possible to build in this locality."

A dome atop it had an iron-grilled balcony fit for an appearance by Zorro. A garden court with fountain, flowers, and shrubbery fronted it. Sidewalks bordered the court on three sides, the hotel's long inlaid porch on the fourth. Concrete floors, steam heat, every room an outside room each with a closet and washstand, 26 showers, and eight bathtubs, made it modern by 1923 standards.

The lobby, which had terraza magnatile floors and leather upholstered furniture, was the most impressive interior feature. At the far end of the lobby was the front desk and office, on both sides of which were stairs to a well-lighted foyer on the second floor. Near the glass front doors stood the telegraph office, and to the left were glass doors into the sunken dining room. The latter had enamel walls and an

oak floor and could accommodate over 200 people.

Owners asked the community to name it. Suggestions poured in: Casa Grande, Oregon; Oregon Villa; Oregon Trail Lodge; Oregon Palace Hotel; Central Oregon Hotel; Ochoco Palace Hotel; Ochoco Beauty; The Pioneer; Pioneer Fountain Hotel; Rimrock Inn; Juniper Inn; The Oriental; Blue Mountain Inn; Takena Inn; Hotel Prineville; and Menepa. The Portland Chamber of Commerce recommended The Ochoco and local petitions supported the Ochoco Inn.

On Monday, August 13, 1923, the $200,000 Ochoco Inn opened for business, managed by Mrs. McDowell. For decades it was the pride of Prineville and few profiles of the little town failed to mention its Spanish-style hotel. The Oregon Cattlemen's Association located its state headquarters in one of the hotel stores.

Owners failed to maintain the hotel very well and the upstairs soon acquired a seedy look, but they kept the downstairs facilities in good condition and these became a center of community activity. People wishing a good view of a parade or to just sit and chat with friends while watching traffic would find no better place for it than the shaded front porch of the Ochoco Inn. One day each year, Santa Claus sat there, a line of

waiting children snaking across the porch and down the sidewalks.

Spencer Tracy spent a night there, and in May 1952 some local Democrats paid $5 a plate to eat in the hotel dining room with Presidential contender Estes Kefauver. Not all guests behaved properly. A couple of rowdy cowboys tossed off all their clothes one night to go skinny dipping in the fountain. And memories still linger of goings-on at a convention held there in the 'twenties.

It all ended about 3 am one cold morning in late August 1966. A fire erupted in the kitchen, spread rapidly up the vents, and reached the roof. The roof had been tarred and retarred so often that now a 8- to 12-inch layer of tar covered it — explosive fuel.

Firemen found the dining room and roof in flames, the rest of the building full of smoke. Soon they needed airpacks to go beyond the lobby. A Redmond tanker arrived to help Prineville firefighters who eventually poured four million gallons of water on the fire. But it soon became obvious the building could not be saved. For some it triggered memories of 44 years earlier. Before the fire was controlled, the hotel and more than $500,000 worth of property had perished.

Smoke still rose from the rubble when people began to talk of rebuilding. Prineville residents wanted the Ochoco Inn back. They wanted it rebuilt to look the same as it had looked before the fire. After months passing without action, residents were saying they would be satisfied to have a hotel of any sort on the property. After several years passed, they were saying they would be satisfied just to have the enormous burned-out ruin torn down and cleared away.

Finally in 1972 new owners of the property completed plans to open a motel and restaurant on the site. Workers removed the ruin and in 1973 the Colovos family opened the Ochoco Inn and Cinnabar Restaurant. Although it lacked the old Ochoco Inn's splendid lobby, travelers found its rooms a vast improvement over its predecessor's and the Cinnabar became such a popular meeting place that today is probably better known than the motel.

Most communities in Oregon have had hotels. But those in Prineville had produced some unique — often unpleasant, true, but unique — history. ■

The Johnny Appleseed of the Northwest

*The multi-million dollar Oregon fruit raising industry
can trace its beginnings to an Iowa farmer with wanderlust.*

By Francis X. Sculley

In the late 1830s, Henderson Lewelling had established a large fruit nursery in Henry County, Iowa, profitable enough that he was able to afford an imposing yellow limestone house. But like Johnny Appleseed, he was a natural wanderer. He began to hear wondrous tales of the fertile land of the Willamette Valley in Oregon and so, by 1845, had decided to close out his nursery and move to Oregon. In the spring of 1847, he built a special covered wagon with two boxes filled with a compost of charcoal and dirt set in the bottom. Into these, he set his stock of young apple trees, pears, quince, plums, cherries, grapes, and berries. In all, there were about 700 plants ranging from 20 inches to four feet in height. He also laid in a supply of fruit seeds. On April 17, 1847, with seven wagons in his party, he and his family set out for Oregon. Beyond the Missouri, the little party joined a wagon train, the common arrangement for safety.

But his traveling nursery was an impediment to the wagon train. The wagon, loaded with nursery stock, was heavy. It moved slowly. The oxen were worn to a nub getting the ponderous wagon over the mountains. The heat was unbearable. The oxen grew lame. Worse yet, Lewelling's partner died of cholera somewhere along the Sweetwater River. Then two of his oxen died. Irritation grew among the other wagons in the train because the men felt that his load was holding up the progress of the train. They implored him to throw away his nursery stock as it would be impossible to cross the mountains under such a handicap. Lewelling refused. In the end, he had to leave the train alone with his seven wagons.

He watered his trees everyday, no matter how scarce the water. Half of his trees died, but the rest were in full leaf. Remarkably, they saved the life of the party when indians attacked. So amazed were the warriors at the green growth, they felt the caravan was under the special care of the Great Spirit and so withdrew in wonder.

In October, Lewelling reached The Dalles in Oregon, transferred his stock to a boat, and floated down the Columbia River. On November 17th, seven months after leaving Iowa, he reached the Willamette Valley, settled his family in a squatter's cabin and transplanted his nursery stock, some of which had grown three feet along the way. He then planted all of the seed he had brought.

In 1851, the young orchard he had planted began to bear — and heavily. In the meantime, he had been propagating from his stock and was selling to Oregon settlers.

There was an unexpected bonanza. Among the seeds that he had brought with him had been some cherry pits, and among the seedling from these appeared a cherry tree with large and dark colored delicious fruit. Lewelling propagated the variety and named it after a Chinese workman named Bing. It was to become and remains today as the most popular cherry of the Far West.

Henderson Lewelling is generally recognized as the father of Oregon's multi-million dollar fruit raising industry. ■

The Clark Massacre Party of 1851

The rigors and dangers facing the pioneers following the Oregon Trail are again revealed in this tragic and mystifying saga of what became known as the "Clark Massacre."

By Don Burgderfer

When the group of mounted Indian warriors galloped out of the sage and headed for the horse-drawn hack, their intentions were clear. They drew their rifles from leather scabbards and began to shoot at the white people before them. By the time the attackers had left the scene, two of the whites were dead and one was grievously wounded. And thus began the tragic and sometimes mystifying saga of what became known as the "Clark Massacre."

In the spring of 1849, Thomas Clark, aged 33, his brother, James Clark, aged 29, and his two partners, John Magison and Joshua Jackson Vandevert, headed west for the California gold fields. They were well-provisioned and ready to make their fortunes. As a matter of fact, they did do quite well. In the spring of 1850, it was agreed by the partners that Thomas Clark would take a large part of the proceeds and head east by way of the Isthmus. Meanwhile, the others would continue working the successful mine for a while longer.

Their plan was to settle in the Willamette Valley of Oregon, and it was Clark's mission to use their money to buy blooded cattle and horses and return to Oregon with them, by which time the other partners would also have returned to the Valley. According to a descendant

An undated photo of Grace Clark Vandevert, the English girl who was brutally injured by Indians in the 1851 attack in Idaho. She and Joshua Jackson Vandevert married in 1853 and had seven children, one of whom (William P.) started a homestead south of Bend. Grace died in 1875 at the age of 48. Photo from the Clark/Vandevert archives, provided courtesy of Jim and Carol Gardner. Copy of original by Don Burgderfer

of these pioneers, W.P. Vandevert, most of the cattle in the Valley at that time were half-wild, long-horned Spanish types, and the partners felt that they could import and breed much better strains than currently present.

Thomas Clark was an Eng-lish-man and knew his animals well. He was also an avid hunter and bred fine hunting dogs. He traveled throughout the east and midwest purchasing good stock, and by the spring of 1851 had assembled 65 blooded horses and 63 high-quality Durham cattle. By April of 1851 it was time to return home. The Clark cara-van formed up and embarked from Springfield, Illinois, headed for the Willamette Valley via the Oregon Trail.

The party that headed for Oregon was led by Thomas Clark and also included his mother, Elizabeth, 66, his younger brothers, Charles, 30, and Hodgson, 23, his 25-year old sister, Grace, and others who helped drive the cattle. According to the widow Hoffman, who with her son had joined the party, there was a total of six wagons, each drawn by six yoke of oxen. There was also a "hack" or carriage which had been specially built for Clark in St. Louis, and it may have been the very first such vehicle to cross the plains.

Elizabeth and her daughter Grace typically rode ahead of the main group in the hack to locate good campsites for each night, and they were often accompanied by Grace's brother, Hodgson. This habit of the hack being ahead of (and isolated from) the main body of the train was to have very dire consequences later on.

The trip to Fort Hall, Idaho, (near present-day Pocatello) was relatively uneventful. They normally traveled only about twelve miles per day in order to spare the stock any undue stress. From Fort Hall the route would take them along the Snake River toward Fort Boise and Farewell Bend.

At Farewell Bend, the Oregon Trail left the Snake River, headed over a pass toward present-day Huntington and then continued on to La Grande and The Dalles. From The Dalles, one took the Barlow Road (opened in 1846) to Oregon City and points beyond.

Sometime around August 6, 1851, the Clark party had gotten about 40 miles west of Fort Hall, Idaho, and had arrived near the confluence of the Raft and Snake Rivers. On this day, Thomas Clark had ridden ahead of the group and had located a fine looking campsite for the night, near Black Rock Creek.

Thomas rode back to the hack and told Elizabeth, Grace and Hodgson about his find. Then, he took his dogs and shotgun and rode up the nearby Raft River to do some duck hunting. The hack, being in the lead as usual, arrived at the place Mr. Clark had mentioned and Grace and Hodgson climbed down. Their mother, Elizabeth, never had a chance to alight, because about 30 Snake Indians had chosen this opportune moment to attack the lead elements of the Clark train.

The Clarks had heard earlier that the Bannock and Shoshone (Snake) Indians were stealing cattle from the emigrant parties. That being the case, commentators of that time wondered why the train hadn't kept in closer formation and maintained better security. Said one early writer, "The disaster to the Clarks was the result of imprudence." In any event, the bulk of the Indian raiders headed for the lead horses and cattle, which was their real objective, but about eight broke off and went

The Clarks had heard earlier that the Bannock and Shoshone (Snake) Indians were stealing cattle from the emigrant parties. That being the case, commentators of that time wondered why the train hadn't kept in closer formation and maintained better security.

This photo of Joshua Jackson Vandevert was taken by the same studio in Eugene and probably at the same time as the portrait of Grace. After wife Grace died in 1875, Joshua left the valley and homesteaded on the north slope of the Powell Buttes. He died in 1910 at age 87 and is buried in Prineville.
Photo from the Clark/Vandevert archives, provided courtesy of Jim and Carol Gardner. Copy of original by Don Burgderfer

for the hack, rifles unsheathed, ready for mayhem. They especially wanted the beautiful Morgan horses pulling that rig.

The accounts of what happened next vary a bit in detail from writer to writer, but in sifting through the various narratives, the following seems to be a fair picture of the violent events that unfolded.

The young Grace Clark and her mother, Elizabeth, must have been terror-stricken as the dust clouds arose from the attacking horsemen. Warlike yells and shouts were uttered as hooves pounded the ground around them, and soon the dust was mixed with the acrid, unmistakable smell of black gunpowder.

The first to die was Hodgson, who was trying to reach for his rifle inside the hack when several balls struck him and one pierced his heart. When the Indians had first been sighted, Elizabeth told him to round up the loose horses and drive them back to the main wagon train. But, he had seen the rifles being drawn out of their scabbards. Said the 23-year old, "Now, Mother, I am not going to leave you and Grace. These Indians mean mischief. I am going to stay here and protect you." This young hero's gallant bravery cost him his life, and his murderers subsequently crushed his skull with rocks.

Apparently, the Indians perceived no real threat from the two surviving women. So, they started unhitching the hack's beautiful horses. That was when Elizabeth or Grace screamed at them in protest and outrage. Grace started to climb back up into the hack and put her arm around her mother to protect her from harm. The Indians reacted by firing at the women. One of the three balls received by Elizabeth passed through Grace's wrist, according to several accounts. And one of these went on to pierce Elizabeths body for a fatal wound. (One account says she died instantly as a ball pierced her heart, but another says she survived until 7 pm that evening.)

Now wounded in the wrist, the frantic and terrified Grace tried to climb down out of the hack. Other shots were fired and one ball caught her under the armpit and passed clear through her body. (One report suggests that the ball probably passed between her lungs and vertebrae, thus avoiding the type of extensive tissue destruction that a more modern, high-velocity projectile might have inflicted.) It was said that Grace's wound did not heal fully until part of a bullet patch finally worked its way out about a year later.

Some reports tell of Grace, Hodgson and Elizabeth being struck by arrows as well as bullets, but there is no definitive record of this happening.

The attackers were brutal, ripping off Grace's clothes, throwing her down the river embankment (during which one account says her leg was fractured) and then pummeling her with large stones. At some point, according to popular accounts, the Indians also started to scalp her. Whether it was from the rocks thrown down upon her or from a scalping, she bore those scars for the rest of her life. (Of interest is the fact that despite many reports of the partial scalping of Grace, her son, William P. Vandevert, did not mention it in a 1922 interview regarding the massacre. He attributed her scars to the rocks.)

If scalping was in progress, it ended abruptly as a large cloud of dust was seen approaching the massacre site. It was Thomas Clark, who had heard the shooting and was racing to the rescue with his dogs. The Indians thought it was a large mounted party and quickly left the area, but not without the prized Morgan horses they coveted.

Soon, the main body of the Clark train arrived, the dead were secretively buried, and the dazed group considered what their next move should be. A dispatch was sent forward to other parties ahead of the Clark train, and a dozen or so men responded. From the combined groups assembled, a party of sixteen men, led by Charles Clark, Thomas' brother, was formed to pursue the

Indians and punish them. After tracking about 15 miles in a northeasterly direction they did find the Indians, but in the ensuing battle one of the pursuers was killed and another seriously wounded.

The Indians had ensconced themselves in an almost impregnable natural fortress, and could not be dislodged. It was said that they even raised a black flag and cursed at the hapless pioneers who confronted them. It was also reported that not all of the "savages" were Indians. In fact, it was claimed that the band was led by several men with long, sandy-colored beards. These were obviously renegade whites, a fairly common occurrence in the pioneer west. Grace was said to have later commented, "I looked into the face of an attacker and I looked into blue eyes!"

The Indian band was also accompanied by a large number of stolen cattle and horses, including some of those just taken from the Clarks. Further assaults on the Indians were considered fruitless and the dreary men returned to their camp with their dead and wounded comrades. There was little to be done now but to continue the trip to Oregon's Willamette Valley. (Eleven years later, in August of 1862, a wagon train of 25 families was attacked by Indians a few miles east of here, leaving ten dead at what is now known as Massacre Rocks.)

Twenty-five year old Grace Clark was fully expected to die. Her wounds were so grave that few humans would survive such injury. Yet, she persisted in life. After several days of waiting for her expected demise, the pioneers decided to comfort her as best they could in one of the wagons and push on. This courageous young English girl from Yorkshire County must have been all grit and tough as boot leather. She was comforted in one of the wagons by women of the caravan and also attended by a Dr. Cloud from another party in the train. (Grace's son, W.P. Vandevert, later said that Cloud may not have been a real doctor, but was instead a school teacher with a limited knowledge of first aid.) In any event, since Grace did survive, Cloud must have done something right!

One of the women who took loving care of Grace was a cousin, Jane Coultas Evans, whose original journals of the 1851 trip were burned in a fire. In 1904 this 80-year old lady reconstructed some

Twenty-five year old Grace Clark was fully expected to die. Her wounds were so grave that few humans would survive such injury. Yet, she persisted in life. This courageous young English girl from Yorkshire County must have been all grit and tough as boot leather.

of her memories in a diary which was later found by Evans' granddaughter. Jane told of holding Grace and trying to comb her tangled, blood-matted hair while the train resumed its westward journey. (It appears that Cloud wanted to simply cut her hair, but Evans resisted such a drastic measure.)

By the middle of September, 1851, the Clark train reached its Willamette Valley destination, and the survivors went about the more mundane business of carving a new niche for themselves in their adopted Oregon homeland. It was surely with mixed feelings that these folks finally ended their journey to Oregon. They had just traveled over "the longest cemetery in America," a 2,000-mile stretch which by 1862 averaged one grave for every one-tenth mile!

The Clarks arrived in Oregon without the prized stock that had been stolen, but Thomas and Charles went back east again in 1852 and returned with more stock as part of the 1853 "Lost Wagon Train of Elijah Elliott, which travels a new cut-off route straight across Central Oregon to Bend. (See page 44 for the story of that pioneer saga.)

The other mining partners had returned to Oregon just prior to the Clark Massacre; and while there was sadness and disappointment over the loss of lives and stock, it was not a total loss in the eyes of one partner, Joshua J. Vandevert. For Thomas Clark had brought to Oregon a prize of great value — his sister, Grace Clark. Grace in time recovered from her terrible wounds; and on April 14, 1853, she and Joshua (better known as "Jack") Vandevert were married and took up residence at Jack's homestead near Cottage Grove. (Contrary to some accounts, at no time did Grace ever live anywhere in Central Oregon).

The story goes that Joshua was actually named "Vandervort" at the time he and Grace were married. However, Grace decided that it sounded too "dutchy" to her and pronounced that henceforth it would be "Vandevert." What Joshua said at that time is not recorded, but he forthwith became a Vandevert.

Jack and Grace had seven children, the first of which was William Plutarch Vandevert, born February 24, 1854. It was this son who settled a homestead on the Little Deschutes River south of Bend in 1892. Before that, he had married Sadie

It was surely with mixed feelings that these folks finally ended their journey to Oregon.

They had just traveled over "the longest cemetery in America," a 2,000-mile stretch which by 1862 averaged one grave for every one-tenth mile!

Vincentheller in Texas, and they eventually had eight children. Three of those children became physicians; and two of them (Clint and George) had practices in Bend, while the third, Arthur, set up his practice in Indiana.

One of the most endearing of the Vandevert clan was Katherine Grace, who was born in 1890 and died of influenza in 1918. She is buried by Little River. She was highly literate and intelligent, but (unlike her brothers) was denied medical school. Katherine's lyrical diaries speak of both happiness and much disappointment. As Carol Gardner told me, " She was a mighty unhappy girl."

On February 20, 1875, at age 48, Grace Clark Vandevert died in the Valley. On January 18, 1992, her granddaughter, Ruth Vandevert Lane, informed me that "What really eventually killed Grace was an old bullet wound in her lung that never quite healed." Ironically, this amazing lady, who had been so severely brutalized by the Shoshones in 1851, had devoted much of her life to giving aid to indigent Indians in the Willamette Valley!

After Grace's death, her husband, Joshua, moved to Central Oregon and homesteaded on the northern slope of Powell Butte. His huge white barn still stands there and is a well-known landmark. At about age 87, Joshua died at his son Bill's Little River ranch on July 18, 1910 and was buried in Prineville. W.P.'s wife Sadie lived until 1924, and Bill (W.P.) until 1944. Both passed away

in Bend. W.P. and Sadie's son Claude took over the Little River ranch upon the death of his father.

When Claude died in 1975, his wife Jeanie took over the maintenance of the ranch. Several years ago she sold the ranch to Jim and Carol Gardner, who now live on the "Old Homestead" and are beautifully restoring it. In addition, the Gardners have gathered vast amounts of material about the Clark/Vandevert clan and are working on a comprehensive history of the family.

There is another important part of the Clark Massacre tale that we haven't touched upon yet: the never-ending controversy over which route the party followed to the Valley after the massacre, and whether or not they really came through Bend. But that will have to be another story!* ■

ACKNOWLEDGMENTS:
Jim and Carol Gardner, now the owners of W.P. Vandevert's "Old Homestead," on Little River, were most helpful in providing this author materials and old family photographs.

Also, my heartfelt thanks go to Grace Ann Vandevert McNellis, of Gig Harbor, WA, for her invaluable provision of genealogical and historical material on the Clark and Vandevert families. She is truly the family history buff and is also the source of many of the materials that the Gardners now archive.

I am also much indebted to Ruth Vandevert Lane of Prineville, Oregon, for her memories and observations regarding the Vandevert family history.

SUGGESTED FURTHER READING:
Bend in Central Oregon – Ray Hatton, 1978
Conversations with Bullwackers,
    Muleskinners, Etc. – Lockley/Helm/1981
"Cutoff Fever" – Leah Collins Menefee
Oregon Historical Quarterlies,
    December 1976 through Spring 1978
    (especially the September 1977 issue)
East of the Cascades – Phil Brogan, 1964
Gold and Cattle Country –
    Herman Oliver & E.R. Jackman, 1961
A History of the Deschutes Country
    in Oregon – Deschutes County Historical
    Society, 1985
" The Lost Wagon Train of Elijah Elliott" –
    Don Burgderfer, Cascades East
    magazine, Fall & Winter issues, 1991
Oregon's Great Basin –
    Denzel & Nancy Ferguson, 1978
Pioneer Roads in Central Oregon –
    Nielsen, Newman & McCart, 1985

*EDITORS NOTE: See the following page for this fascinating story.

The Mystery of the Clark Massacre Party's Journey Through Oregon

Some historians now question whether the Clark party ever really came across central Oregon to Bend in 1851.

This bronze plaque has graced Bend's Pioneer Park for over 63 years. Though it is undeniably difficult to refute something that has been cast in bronze, some historians now question that the Clark party ever really came across Oregon to Bend in 1851.
Photo by Don Burgderfer

By Don Burgderfer

In the spring of 1851, a pioneer party led by Thomas Clark embarked upon the Oregon Trail. Their destination: the Willamette Valley of Oregon. Included in the group were Tom's mother, Elizabeth, two brothers, Charles and Hodgson, and his sister, Grace. In August of 1851, near the confluence of the Raft and Snake Rivers, the party was set upon by marauding Snake Indians bent upon stealing horses and cattle. In the ensuing conflict, Elizabeth, Hodgson and another man were killed, and Grace and another man were severely wounded.

Grace Clark, shot through the wrist and body, and with her head injured by rocks thrown upon her by the Indians, was expected to die. But, she did not. So, after resting several days, the wagons slowly pushed on toward Oregon. The normal Oregon Trail route would take these people along the Snake River to old Fort Boise (near present-day Parma, Idaho). They would then leave the Snake River and head for the Malheur River crossing at present-day Vale. From there, the Oregon Trail went almost due north to Farewell Bend on the Snake River, and thence in a northwesterly direction toward present-day Baker City, La Grande, Pendleton and The Dalles.

West of The Dalles lay the golden treasure – the Willamette Valley. Before 1846, the route there from The Dalles was a tortuous route down the Columbia Gorge, often by crude raft. But, by 1846 the new Barlow Road south of Mt. Hood was being opened up, and this eventually made the trip much easier for the weary pioneers. (See *Cascades East,* Fall & Winter, 1991, for details of the massacre.)

When Thomas Clark stood at the juncture of the Oregon Trail and the Malheur River crossing at Vale in 1851, he had an important decision to make. The problem is, no one is completely certain as to just what that decision was!

Let us consider the mystifying question of what the Clark party did *after* the terrible events of the August massacre on the Snake River. The truth is, there is considerable puzzle-

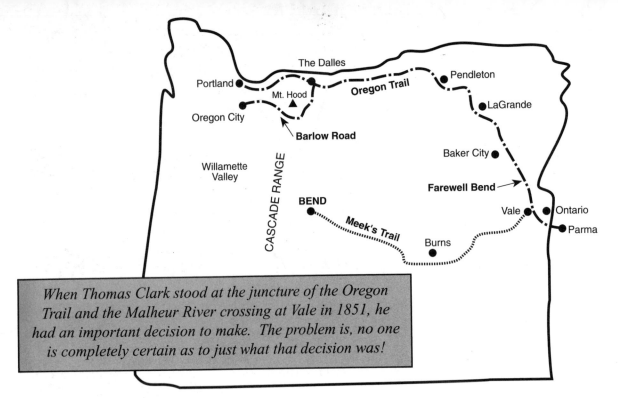

ment and fundamental disagreement on what *route* the Clark train took to the Willamette Valley after the massacre.

There are many descendants of Grace Clark, and in Central Oregon the most notable of these are members of the Vandevert family, which had a well-known homestead just south of present-day Sunriver. This is a family bound together by strong family traditions, and among those traditions are the tales of the epic journey of some of their ancestors, the Clark massacre party of 1851.

The standard legend is that the 1851 Clark Massacre party left Idaho near Fort Boise and went to Vale's Malheur River crossing. At that location they left the traditional Oregon Trail and struck out almost due west across the central part of Oregon until they arrived at present-day Bend. Here they rested awhile and then headed north to connect up the Barlow Road to the Valley. In this version, the assumption has been that the train took up the old Stephen Meek tracks of 1845 (the trail of Blue Bucket fame) and followed those tracks to Bend. To many people, the story is even *more* specific: that the Clark party camped in the present-day Pioneer Park area of Bend until Grace had recovered sufficient strength to continue the journey to the Valley.

Further weight has been given to this version by the presence of a bronze plaque in Pioneer Park. It was dedicated by city fathers on December 7, 1928, and reads as follows: "In 1851 the immigrant trains used this spot to ford the Deschutes River on their trek to western Oregon. Upon departing, the earliest known train named it Farewell Bend and it is from this origin that the present City of Bend derived its name." While the Clark party is not mentioned by name on the plaque, it is the only major party thought to have come to Bend in 1851.

Though it is undeniably difficult to refute something that has been cast in bronze, some historians now question that the Clark party ever really came across Oregon to Bend in 1851. And this is in the face of numerous interviews with

descendants of Grace Clark, including her oldest son, William, who have repeated the accepted "Bend" version time after time through the years!

Let's examine this controversy among historians.

There's hardly a Clark/Vandevert descendant worth the name that won't steadfastly uphold the version that the Clark party *did* come directly across central Oregon to Bend. Said Grace's oldest son, Wm. P. Vandevert, in a 1922 interview: "The train bore southward toward the Three Sisters. They were the first party to pass over the site of what is now Bend. Thomas Clark named Pilot Butte. They came pretty well to the foothills of the Cascades and then swung north, crossing the mountains by the Barlow Trail and coming on down into the Willamette Valley." There isn't much equivocation in *those* words!

On the other hand, an historian such as Leah Collins Menefee suggests that there has been a gross confusion between the events of the 1851 Clark party and the presence of the very same Thomas and Charles Clark in the subsequent 1853 Elliott "lost" wagon train, a train which most certainly *did* come to the Bend area. And, there are other reasons advanced that question the widely accepted belief that the post-massacre Clark party came across Oregon to Bend in 1851.

For one thing, consider the prior experience of the ill-fated Meek train of 1845. It was well known that those elements which took the usual Oregon Trail route from Vale's Malheur River crossing (instead of Meek's ill-advised cutoff) arrived at The Dalles weeks ahead of the innovative parties that tried a cross-country route through central Oregon. The Meek train had turned into a rebellious disaster near Wagontire, splintering off into various factions that, over a period of time, finally found their way to The Dalles, but not without great suffering and casualties. All of this was known to subsequent trekkers who came west. Including the Clark brothers, we might reasonably assume.

There are those who say that the 1851 Clark party followed

HISTORIC
OREGON TRAIL

FAREWELL BEND

THE LAST CAMP ON THE
WEARY JOURNEY ACROSS
THE SNAKE RIVER PLAINS.
HERE THE OREGON TRAIL
LEFT THE SNAKE RIVER
AND WOUND OVERLAND TO
THE COLUMBIA. HERE CAMP-
ED WILSON PRICE HUNT,
DECEMBER 23, 1811; CAPT.
BONNEVILLE, JANUARY 10,
1834; NATHANIEL J. WYETH,
AUGUST 25, 1834; LT. JOHN C.
FREMONT, OCTOBER 13, 1845.

Shimmering in the distance is the large bend in the Snake River at Farewell Bend. Here the wagon trains of the Old Oregon Trail left the river and headed uphill toward our camera and thence to The Dalles. LEFT: This historical marker is at Farewell Bend State Park on the Snake River. Did the Clark Massacre party of 1851 camp in this vicinity, or did they camp at the Farewell Bend area of present-day Bend? Photos by Don Burgderfer

the 1845 Meek tracks across Oregon to Bend. However, Keith Clark, a local historian who extensively researched and wrote a book on the Meek saga *(The Terrible Trail)* expressed doubts to me that *any* of the Meek splinter groups came directly to Bend or left any tracks that would have led another wagon train all the way to that specific location.

When Tom Clark did reach the Malheur Crossing, he may well have wondered, as did many pioneers, if there wasn't a shorter route directly west across the Oregon wilderness to the Valley. (Several years later, in 1853, such a route *was* implemented by the Elliott "lost wagon train" party, with *much* difficulty.)

Now, try to put yourself into Tom Clark's boots. You *know* what happened to the Meek party and their tribulations and how much *longer* it took them to get to The Dalles. *Your* party has just been through a devastating Indian attack. Stock and draft animals are now in short supply. Three people,

including your mother and brother, have been killed. Two people, your beloved sister Grace and one of the men, are seriously wounded and in need of medical assistance.

Will you, as the leader of your party, leave Malheur Crossing on the known, well-traveled Oregon Trail to The Dalles? Or, will you now select the discredited Meek trail which led to the well-known travail in that 1845 debacle?

Would *you* select the old Meek route, knowing that it is a trail whose path is generally obscure, with water and forage supplies quite uncertain? Would you select this route knowing of the well-publicized rebellion against Meek when his "route" became mired in doubt and uncertainty? And, finally, would you take your now-diminished party over a lonely, untraveled route which most certainly guarantees further contact with armed and murderous hostiles? Not to mention, a route which guarantees no further medical help for your sister?

Which route do *you* think Thomas Clark would have chosen? Again, I must warn you, it is entrenched in the family legend that he did *not* choose the traditional, proven Oregon Trail route to The Dalles. Rather, he chose the nebulous Meek trail of 1845 and somehow made it to the Bend area.

There is, however, a disturbing letter that Thomas Clark, himself, wrote on August 7, 1902. In this letter, he mentions meeting brother James (who by then had returned to Oregon from his 49'er California gold exploits) "about 30 miles *east* of The Dalles." It is assumed by some historians that this letter does pertain to events that happened near the conclusion of the ill-fated 1851 journey. James and Thomas apparently completed financial transactions concerning purchase of some hoofed stocked during this meeting on the Oregon Trail. And Grace Clark, who by now was thankfully "on the mend" was entrusted with a financial note to be later conveyed to a seller in Portland.

Many years after the massacre, in 1901, Linwood Clark (James' son and Thomas' nephew) wrote an account of James' unusual adventures in meeting the 1851 Clark party on the *old* Oregon Trail *east of The Dalles,* and that account fully supported what Thomas Clark later wrote in 1902!

The above information clearly does not coincide with the long-held supposition that the Clark party traveled north from Bend to the Barlow Road. Even in pioneer days, heading from Bend to the Barlow Road would not take one even *close* to "30 miles east of The Dalles" on the Old Oregon Trail.

Also, wouldn't leaving the usual, established Oregon Trail for a different one have been quite a remarkable and noteworthy event in the lives of these wagon train participants? Yet, in none of the known journals of this train's participants is there any mention of any deviation from the regular Oregon Trail route to the Valley. The Meek and (later) Elliott trains found the so-called "cut-off" route to be *quite* noteworthy!

There is some other evidence, something the lawyers might label "circumstantial" in nature. One must infer from it. But, it is simply this: In the fall of 1853, the "lost" Elliott wagon train was making its way west on a short-cut across central Oregon (a route which, initially, often followed the Stephen Meek trail of 1845.) The train encountered greater and greater difficulties (see *Cascades East,* 1991 Fall and Winter editions). About the middle of September, 1853, eight riders left the Elliott train on a rescue mission to go on to the Valley over the new "cut-off" trail and obtain Valley residents' help for the immigrants.

The nominal leader of this rescue group of eight men was none other than Charles Clark! He was probably considered the leader because he was, at 32, older than the other seven men. This is the same party that got totally turned around for *four* days after leaving the Elliott train before they finally headed out in the correct westerly direction toward Bend!

It seems odd that Charles, having supposedly been over this same ground several years before, should suddenly become so confused as to his location.

This is the same rescue party that did arrive in the Bend area and then, in their search for their Diamond Peak pass over the Cascades, ascended with great effort the saddle between the South and Middle Sisters mountains, thinking that *this* was Diamond Peak. And from there they were able to see that the *real* Diamond Peak was many miles to the South!

It has been suggested that *if* Charles Clark, as the story persists, had come to Bend with the 1851 Clark massacre party, his mistakes in guiding the 1853 rescue party would not have occurred.

It does appear that Charles Clark had very little familiarity with the central Oregon area or the (now) Bend area. Yet, this is where he was supposed to have camped in 1851 (according to accepted tradition) while Grace recovered from her serious wounds. It also seems reasonable to assume that Clark had never seen either Diamond Peak or the Three Sisters from the east side of the mountains, since they would hardly be confused with one another.

Meanwhile, *Thomas* Clark was also a member of the 1853 Elliott train. He was, in fact, bringing out to Oregon a second shipment of stock to replace those that had been stolen by the Indians in 1851. When the train had arrived at the Silvies

There is a suspicion that part of the problem of knowing what route the 1851 Clark party took results from a confusion of names. In effect, there were two Farewell Bends! The members of the 1851 Clark massacre party undoubtedly mentioned camping at a "Farewell Bend"... but which one?

River, Elijah Elliott had said that they should continue to follow the old Meek tracks westward, along the *northern* shores of Malheur and Harney Lakes. Elliott was correct about the northern route he preferred. But the members of the train (including Tom Clark, we might assume) insisted on taking what turned out to be the much more arduous *southern* route. It was a time-consuming mistake which anyone with any familiarity with the terrain would have strenuously objected to.

If Thomas Clark had, in fact, been over this route in 1851, one has to wonder why there is no record of his support for Mr. Elliott's wiser choice of a northern route above the lakes. On this matter, the record is silent.

There is a suspicion that part of the problem of knowing *what* route the 1851 Clark party took results from a confusion of names. In effect, there were *two* Farewell Bends! One was on the Snake River. *This* Farewell Bend was the place where immigrants on the Oregon Trail left the Snake River and headed northwest through a pass in the hills toward what is now Huntington and on to Durkee, on the Burnt River. Thence the old trail proceeded past Baker and La Grande and Pendleton and on toward The Dalles.

But, there was also the *other* Farewell Bend, where pioneers left a pronounced double bend in the Deschutes River and headed north or south (but *never* west) depending on their destination. This was the future Central Oregon townsite of Bend. The members of the 1851 Clark massacre party undoubtedly mentioned camping at a "Farewell Bend"... but, *which* one? Some of the narratives almost wax poetic as they picture the rapture with which Grace Clark beheld the joys of camping by a cool, bubbling stream. But, where was she, really?

As for the plaque in Bend's Pioneer Park, even *that* has been called into question. In 1940 a descendant of one of the early Bend-area pioneers was interviewed by the Bend *Bulletin* newspaper. His name was Linsy Sisemore. Here is

Continued on page 21